KEYS TO READING
AN ANNUAL REPORT

George Thomas Friedlob, Ph. D., C. P. A.
and
Ralph E. Welton, Ph. D.

School of Accountancy
Clemson University
Clemson, South Carolina

BARRON'S

New York • London • Toronto • Sydney

All inquiries should be addressed to:
Barron's Educational Series, Inc.
250 Wireless Boulevard
Hauppauge, New York 11788

Library of Congress Catalog Card No. 88-34268

International Standard Book No. 0-8120-3930-0

Library of Congress Cataloging in Publication Data

Friedlob, George Thomas.
    Keys to reading an annual report.

    1. Financial statements. I. Welton, Ralph E.
II. Title.
HF5681.B2F773 1989   657'.3   88-34268
ISBN 0-8120-3930-0

PRINTED IN THE UNITED STATES OF AMERICA

9012 9770 98765432

CONTENTS

SECTION I - UNDERSTANDING ANNUAL REPORT COMPONENTS

SECTION II - UNDERSTANDING FINANCIAL STATEMENTS

SECTION III - ANALYZING FINANCIAL STATEMENTS

1

UNDERSTANDING THIS BOOK

This book is organized in 50 short keys. Each offers an immediately practical explanation of some vital aspect of annual reporting. The text is designed to be read either straight through or in random order, selecting topics as questions arise. If you do not understand the significance of long-term debt, for instance, you can simply look it up. There is a key on long-term (noncurrent) debt, another key specifically devoted to bonds and amortization, and still another key on debt and equity that will assist you in evaluating the company's level of long-term borrowing. Consult the index as a cross-reference to determine what subjects are covered in all the keys.

The book concludes with a list of questions and answers—the very questions (we hope) that you might ask us if we were close friends or business associates. Reading through this section is a good way to obtain an overview of the book and the basics of understanding annual reports.

Understanding accounting and financial reporting are formidable yet achievable learning objectives. The Securities and Exchange Commission (SEC), the Financial Accounting

Standards Board, and various committees of the American Institute of Certified Public Accountants have promulgated volumes of principles, standards, and rules to organize and regiment the financial reporting of businesses in the United States. To help you through this maze, the following keys are arranged to proceed through three levels:

1. Understanding the annual report components;
2. Understanding the financial statements contained in an annual report, and
3. Analyzing the financial statements using ratio analysis.

Excerpts from actual annual reports are used to illustrate points made in the text. In addition, it's a good idea to have an annual report at your side as you go through the keys. Read about current assets, then examine the current assets section of your financial report. Study depreciation methods, then look to see which methods your company uses.

This book is intended to be a working reference. Read it and prosper.

2

WHAT IS AN ANNUAL REPORT?

The key to understanding an annual report is to realize that it is designed to satisfy the information needs of many different people with many different needs. Stockholders, creditors, potential stockholders, potential creditors, economists, financial analysts, suppliers, and customers all look to the same published annual report to satisfy their information needs.

The heart of an annual report is the financial statements, which must conform to accounting and reporting standards established by the Financial Accounting Standards Board (FASB), the Securities and Exchange Commission (SEC), and various committees of the American Institute of Certified Public Accountants (AICPA). The requirements of these different groups are a mixed blessing. Because financial statements are very structured, by both convention and legal requirements, they are not tailored to meet the needs of any one group precisely. Each group of users may find something lacking. But because of the high degree of structure and the involvement of the Certified Public Accountant (CPA), readers of financial statements can rely on the fair presentation of

7

the information they receive. Thus, we can review the financial statements of a company in New York or California and decide to buy stock, to lend money, or in some other way to become involved with the company, when we do not know any of the managers and have never seen the company's factory. Of course, there is always the possibility of outright fraud. Even experienced auditors can be fooled by unscrupulous operators.

A large company may spend over half a million dollars to have an independent CPA audit the financial statements, and another fortune to have the assembled annual report published and distributed. Designing and printing annual reports, with all their glossy pictures and graphs and colors, has become an industry in itself. Of course, the best-looking reports are not always the most informative reports. This book will help you distinguish the pertinent facts from the glossy presentation.

Most of this book will be concerned with explaining the keys to understanding the various facets of the financial statements. The next few sections, however, will focus on the contents of the annual report other than the accounting requirements of the financial statements.

3

HIGHLIGHTS, LETTER, AND REVIEW

When you pick up an annual report and begin to page through it, you will notice that the financial statements (the dull-looking pages) are toward the back. The front pages of an annual report, in contrast, are frequently beautiful, with full-color artwork and photographs. It is this glossy part of the report that management controls; accountants control the drab, rear portion. Management's part of the annual report typically consists of three sections:

1. Annual Report Highlights. This section contains highlights of the company's operations, financial statements, stock performance, or whatever else management wishes to present. This section frequently includes graphs or tables to display the favorable trends management wishes to publicize. Generally, this section will also contain statements of the company's sales, profits, and earnings per share for several years. As you read through the keys on the following pages, you will become familiar with most of the terms and concepts introduced in the highlights.

2. Letter to Shareholders. "I am pleased to report (or inform or otherwise convey) . . ." is a common beginning for this section. The letter is from the president or both the president and the chairman of the board, and usually his or her (or their) smiling photograph accompanies the letter. The key to understanding the letter to shareholders is to ask "What do I expect them to say?" and "What did they really say?" The letter will contain the self-congratulatory, optimistic message you expect. That much is usually obvious. But it can be difficult to figure out what they are really saying. Vague wording, colorful adjectives, and meaningless euphemisms are frequently used to conceal the fact that, in truth, the managers are not telling you anything at all.

3. Review of Operations. This section usually consumes the largest part of the annual report and is designed primarily to impress the reader. The company may dwell on its products or its many locations in beautiful settings—whatever management and the public relations folks decide is effective. Most of the photographs and artwork will be in this section. You may enjoy it. But believe it only with caution!

4

FINANCIAL STATEMENTS AND NOTES

At the heart of an annual report are the financial statements. The minimum report consists of a balance sheet, income statement, statement of cash flows, and the accompanying notes and auditor's opinion. All of these sections are analyzed in subsequent keys. The notes are often as important and informative as the statements themselves. These notes are largely descriptive and include information on such things as accounting methods, commitments, noncurrent liabilities and their due dates, inventory components, employee pension provisions, and a number of other disclosures.

The independent auditor's opinion is a short report addressed to the shareholders of the company, giving the auditor's opinion on the financial statements prepared by management. An unqualified opinion is good. Any other opinion is less than good. Qualified opinions, which contain the phrase "except for," should put you on guard. The entire auditor's opinion and a discussion of the types of opinions an auditor can give are discussed in Keys 5 and 9.

A number of supplementary tables may accompany an annual report, including:

Reporting by divisions or other principal segments of the business

Financial reporting and changing prices

Five-year summary of operations

Summary of quarterly figures for current and previous year

Management's discussion and analysis section is required by the Securities and Exchange Commission. Management is required to discuss all developments affecting three key areas of the company's business: (1) results of operations, (2) capital resources, and (3) liquidity. In addition, management is required to discuss all past and future conditions and uncertainties that may materially affect the business. This section is not produced by the public relations department. You may find it informative.

5

BASIC ACCOUNTING PRINCIPLES

Basic accounting principles are the rules and assumptions that underlie financial reporting. These principles tell accountants what items to measure and when and how to measure them. The basic accounting principles can be categorized as follows: (1) the accounting entity, (2) measurement of resources and obligations, (3) periodicity, (4) historical cost and unit of measure, (5) accrual, (6) substance versus form, (7) conservatism, and (8) materiality. Each of these concepts will be defined and discussed below.

Accounting Entity. The accounting entity is the business unit for which financial statements are being prepared. Corporations and trusts are granted general legal existence separate from their owners, while proprietorships and partnerships are legally an extension of the owners' personal affairs. However, even in these latter two cases, accountants view the personal affairs of the owners as separate from the business. For unless each business unit is viewed separately, it is impossible to determine if a commercial venture has been profitable. An accounting entity may also be composed of a parent company and its majority-owned subsidiaries.

Measurement of Resources and Obligations. Business resources are those things of value that the business possesses and can use to produce a profit. The accounting term for resources is *assets*. Obligations, or *liabilities*, are amounts owed to nonowners of the business. The difference between assets and liabilities is the owners' interest (*equity*) in the business. This sum includes their personal investment (*contributed capital*) plus any profits earned by the business and not paid out to the owners (*retained earnings*). A set of financial statements contains measures of assets, liabilities, and owners' equity at the end of the fiscal period (in the balance sheet), and changes that have occurred in assets, liabilities, and owners' equity during the period (in the income statement, statement of retained earnings, and statement of cash flows).

Periodicity. This is the assumption that a company's life must be divided into periods of time in order to measure profit or loss. Ultimately, we can only determine profitability by comparing the owner's interest at the time the business began to their interest at the time of dissolution. Viewing profit or loss at the end of the business's life does not provide timely information for management, investment, or credit decisions. Therefore, accountants divide a company's life into fiscal periods—for example, fiscal year or a fiscal quarter.

Historical Cost and Unit of Measure. This is another measurement concept. Assets and liabilities are recorded in the accounting records at their original or historical cost. For example, if we purchase land for $1 million with a $1 million mortgage, the assets would be increased by $1 million (the land) and the liabilities would be increased by $1 million (the mortgage note). These values will continue in the accounting records until another business event indicates the need for changing them. Examples of such events would include the sale of an asset, the payment of a liability, or the ability to repurchase an asset at less than its historical cost.

The unit of measure employed in financial statements of U.S. based entities is the nominal dollar, unadjusted for inflation or deflation. As a result, one company may have land acquired in 1950 on its books at $100,000, while another company may have a similar piece of property acquired in 1988 recorded on its books at $1 million.

Accrual. The accrual principle attempts to translate into dollars of profit or loss the actual activities of the fiscal period. The accrual principle is a combination of two ideas:

The *revenue recognition* principle provides that revenue (sales price) be recorded when the necessary activities to sell a good or provide a service have been completed. Revenue is recorded at the point of sale regardless of whether cash is collected or a receivable from the customer is created.

The *matching* principle tells the accountant when to record a production cost as expense.

Costs directly associated with producing a certain revenue will be expensed in the same period that the revenue is recorded as earned. Sales commissions are an example of this type of cost because there is a direct association between the sale and the effort of the salesperson.

Other costs are long-lived. They help produce revenue for several periods. Examples include the cost of plant and equipment. The accountant expenses the cost of these types of assets over their expected lives. If a piece of equipment is expected to be used for ten years, its historical cost should be expensed as a cost of revenue production over that same period. This is DEPRECIATION (Key 17).

Other costs are expensed when they arise. These are costs that would not be expected to produce future sales—for example, the cost of heating or cooling a factory.

Under the matching principle an expense can be recorded before, after, or at the time a cost is actually paid. From the accountant's point of view it is the earnings activity that gives rise to the conversion of cost to expense—it does not matter whether that cost has been paid or a liability created.

Substance versus Form. The accountant attempts to report the economic substance of a transaction without regard to its form. For instance, a pledge to United Way is not really a legally binding obligation on the company, but an accountant would record it as a liability. Why? Because the substance of the transaction is that management intends to pay the pledge. The company has made a promise. Its reputation is on the line. Avoiding payment without damaging its reputation is unlikely. The company will choose to pay the pledge.

Conservatism. Conservatism is a downward measurement bias, preferring undervaluation to overvaluation, understatement of income to overstatement of income. The accounting practice of conservatism favors continuing to value assets at their historical cost even though the asset (perhaps land) may be increasing in value each year. Conservatism favors recording losses even before they actually occur if they are considered "likely" to occur. However, the recording of a gain will be postponed until the gain actually occurs even when the gain is considered "likely" to occur (see discussion of Contingencies in Key 7).

Materiality. Materiality deals with relative importance. Considerations of materiality pose the question: Could this item make a difference to the user of the financial statements? A transaction must be accounted for within the measurement and reporting principles known as Generally Accepted Accounting Principles (GAAP; see Key 9) when the amounts involved are judged to be material.

Materiality must be determined by the effect of the transaction on a company's financial statements. When pooled together, as they would be reported in the financial statements, similar transactions involving immaterial amounts may have a material effect. For instance, a large company's purchase of a single microcomputer costing $1500 is not material. Readers of the financial statements may not care if it is expensed or recorded as an asset. But what about 500 microcomputers, purchased at different times during the year? It would be misleading to treat this $750,000 purchase of office equipment as expense in the year of purchase. The computers have a useful life of more than one year and will benefit the company over their useful life. The combined amount of the purchases is material.

6

NOTE ONE

The notes to the financial statements are as important as, if not more important than, the statements themselves. Many times, numbers by themselves do not adequately express *material* information (information that would make a difference to the financial statement user—see Key 5). Notes to the financial statements are largely descriptive and include information on such things as accounting methods, commitments, lease obligations, contingencies, and significant events affecting the company between the end of the fiscal year and the issuance of the annual report. These and other facets of an annual report will be explained in detail as we dissect a typical report in the keys that follow.

Financial reports summarize business transactions in the form of numbers. In some instances, various methods of reporting the same type of transaction have developed. Because these different methods have become popular through use, accountants have had a hard time standardizing reports.

Accounting principles require that if a company has a choice of methods it must disclose the methods used. Most companies list the methods they use in the first note to the financial statements or in a separate section headed Accounting Policies or similar title. For example, different accounting methods exist for valuing inventories and computing depreciation. Acceptable inventory methods include specific identification, FIFO, LIFO, average cost, and lower of cost or market (see Key 15/INVENTORIES for an explanation of these methods). Acceptable depreciation methods include straight-line, units of production, sum-of-the-years' digits, and double-declining balance (see Key 17/DEPRECIATION for an explanation of these methods).

Red Flags. The choice of accounting methods directly affects how the balance sheet is valued and how net income is computed. For example, in the first year of a machine's life, if depreciation is computed on a straight-line basis, it will be less than if it were computed on a sum-of-the-years' digits basis. Since depreciation is essentially a deduction from reported income, the less depreciation, the more income. Conversely, the less depreciation, the more the value reported on the balance sheet for the machine. So both balance sheet and net income figures are directly affected by whatever method of depreciation is used.

Financial statements of a company are not directly comparable, year-to-year, unless the company consistently uses the same valuation methods. (Companies are required to disclose a change in accounting methods; see Key 29/INCOME STATEMENT COMPONENTS.) Direct comparison of financial statements of two different companies is not possible unless they have used the same accounting methods. Note one is very important because it tells us the methods used by the company to prepare its financial statements. As we look at other areas of the financial statements, we will illustrate the major valuation methods so that you can begin to get a feel for their effect on balance sheet valuation and the computation of net income.

7

NOTES ON COMMITMENTS, INCLUDING LEASES AND CONTINGENT LIABILITIES

Commitments. Different types of commitments are entered into by a company. Some commitments directly affect the balance sheet at the time they occur. For example, borrowing $1 million would increase assets $1 million and liabilities by $1 million. But as-yet unexecuted commitments may not be recorded on the balance sheet because they will not have any substantial effect on the company's operations until some time in the future. An example would be a commitment to purchase 5 million parts from a supplier over the next five years. Regardless of whether or not the commitment is recorded on the balance sheet, the principle of materiality requires that the details of all significant commitments be disclosed in the notes to the financial statements.

Some of the common types of commitments disclosed in

financial statements are long-term purchase arrangements, the terms of outstanding loans, agreements to refinance existing debt, lines of credit, lease arrangements, and details of employee pension plans (see Key 8/NOTES RELATING TO PENSIONS). You should pay close attention to these arrangements. Some time in the future they may add to the company's debt structure and increase the amount of cash necessary to meet current obligations.

Leases. Leases are a type of commitment, as indicated above. Some noncancellable long-term leasing arrangements are viewed as alternative purchase and mortgage arrangements. A lease can allow the lessee (party leasing the asset) to retain the asset at the end of the lease. Another lease agreement may set lease payments to cover the purchase price of the asset plus provide the lessor (party providing the asset) with a reasonable return ("interest"). Still another lease may grant the lessee the right to use the asset the majority of its useful life. These leasing arrangements, called capital leases, transfer the risks of ownership to the lessee. Because accountants believe that the economic substance of this type of lease arrangement is the same as an outright purchase of capital assets, they disregard the form of transaction and require it to be recorded as a purchase (see Substance vs. Form in Key 5).

In reporting capital leases, the lessee will record "Property Subject to Capital Leases" as an asset and "Obligations Under Capital Leases" as a liability. The amount recorded as the "historical cost" of the leased asset and the lease obligation is the present value of the required lease payments. Since this is a long-term arrangement, the lease payments must allow the lessors to recover not only their investment in the leased property but a reasonable return—"interest." Deducting this interest from the lease payments gives the "present value" of those payments, which is the value that is recorded as the "historical cost" of both the leased asset and the lease obligation.

The lessee will amortize (see Key 19/DEPLETION AND AMORTIZATION) the leased asset's historical cost over the term of the lease (or over the asset's economic life if the lessee will obtain ownership of the asset at the end of the lease term). Lease payments are divided between principal payments on the recorded lease obligation and interest expense, just as loan payments are divided between payments of principal and interest expense.

Short-term leases and leases that do not transfer the risks of ownership are called operating leases. In these arrangements, the lessees do not record the leased asset or obligation on their balance sheet. All lease payments are recorded as rent expense.

Care should be taken when comparing financial statements of companies that lease to the financial statements of companies that do not lease. All leases give the lessee the benefit of using an asset in exchange for payments at specified intervals. Regardless of whether accounting principles require the lease to be recorded on the balance sheet, the company has a resource to use and an obligation that must be met by cash payments. The financial statement note on leases will provide you with the significant details of lease arrangements and payment schedules. A portion of a note relating to leased assets is shown on the next page.

Contingencies. A contingency exists when the company stands to gain or lose because of a past transaction or event. The amount of gain or loss is "contingent," that is, dependent on another transaction or event. For example, a customer falls in a department store and files a lawsuit. The store owners are now in a contingency situation. The event giving rise to possible loss is the injury of the customer. The amount of loss (if any) will be determined in the future by settlement or court verdict.

All contingencies may be classified by likelihood of outcome: (1) likely to occur, (2) remote chance of occurrence, or (3) may possibly occur. If management, their lawyers, and their accountants believe there is only a remote chance of gain or loss, a contingency will not be disclosed. Where it is possible that a gain or loss will result, the contingency must be disclosed along with management's estimate of the range of possible gain or loss.

Note 8—Lease obligations

The Company leases certain property consisting principally of retail stores, warehouses and transportation equipment under leases expiring through the year 2008. Capital leases are recorded in the Company's balance sheet as assets along with the related debt obligation. All other lease obligations are operating leases, and payments are reflected in the Company's consolidated statement of operations as rental expense. The composition of capital leases reflected as assets in the accompanying consolidated balance sheet is as follows:

	1988	1987
	(in thousands)	
Buildings	$1,236	$1,132
Equipment, furniture and fixtures	2,239	2,375
	3,475	3,507
Accumulated depreciation	2,204	2,006
	$1,271	$1,501

If a contingency is viewed as likely to result in a loss, it must be accrued (the loss is recorded along with an estimated amount of liability). If a single estimate of loss cannot be determined, the smallest amount in management's estimated loss range will be accrued. Footnote disclosures will describe the nature of the contingency and the estimated range of loss.

Contingencies that are likely to result in gain are disclosed but not accrued. This is the principle of conservatism at work. The nature of the gain contingency will be described in the notes to the financial statements.

Notes on contingencies should be evaluated with care. Contingency losses may be time-bombs waiting to blow apart a profitable company. Ask yourself the questions: What will be the impact on the company's cash flow if the possible or likely contingency loss comes to pass? Is the company's debt and liquidity structure capable of handling the loss?

8

NOTES RELATING TO PENSIONS

The key to understanding the cost of employee pension benefits is to realize that the accounting records reflect management's best guess as to what the cost will be. Accountants attempt to measure the cost of these retirement benefits at the time the employee earns them, rather than when the employee actually receives them. Pension expense represents the amount of money management should invest at the end of the year to cover future pension payments that will be made to employees for this additional year's service.

Why is pension cost a best guess? All kinds of assumptions must be made to calculate the required annual investment. Some of these assumptions are: average years of service of an employee at retirement, salary of employee at retirement, number of years an employee is expected to live after retirement, and interest invested funds are expected to earn.

As estimates change, revisions must be made to pension cost. Rather than adjusting the current period's pension expense these revisions will be spread over the current and future accounting periods. Management may choose to invest more or less than the current year's pension expense. If more, the excess funding is recorded in an asset account, Prepaid Pension Cost; if less, it is recorded in a liability account, Unfunded Accrued Pension Cost.

Generally the invested pension funds are handled by a trustee, often a financial institution that specializes in pension investments. The trustee will maintain separate records for the invested funds, and the investment will not be reported on the balance sheet of the employer.

Notes to financial statements disclose the following:

1. Description of pension plan, including groups covered.
2. Type of formula used to calculate retirement benefits.
3. Management's funding policy.
4. The current period's pension expense, indicating amount of prior-service and other costs (1) spread over current and future periods and (2) expensed in current year.
5. A schedule that reconciles management's funding policy with the current value of the invested funds, indicating the amount of prior service cost and cost arising from changes in estimates that have not yet been expensed.

Red Flags. Don't get carried away trying to analyze this material. It is only best-guess information. Many companies do not realize the magnitude of the obligation they are creating every time they increase employee benefits. Like pension benefits, retirement health care benefits granted to employees can be a substantial future obligation. At the present time, companies show expense for the health care benefits actually paid rather than the health care benefits earned by the employees. If a company's work force is young, or if a company does not yet have a large number of retirees, reporting health care benefits paid does not provide good information about the company's future obligation.

Beware of any liability account called Unfunded Projected Benefit Obligation. This means that, given the current rate of earnings, the company's pension fund investments are not enough to cover the future benefits management expects to pay the employees. Likewise, a company that routinely funds less than the current year's pension expense may find itself in trouble down the road.

9

AUDIT REPORTS

The new standard audit report form, adopted by the AICPA in 1988, reads as follows:

We have audited the accompanying balance sheet of X Company as of December 31, 19X1 and the related statements of income, retained earnings, and cash flows for the year then ended. These financial statements are the responsibility of the Company's management. Our responsibility is to express an opinion on these financial statements based on our audit.

We conducted our audit in accordance with generally accepted auditing standards. Those standards require that we plan and perform the audit to obtain reasonable assurance about whether the financial statements are free of material misstatement. An audit includes examining, on a test basis, evidence supporting the amounts and disclosures in the financial statements. An audit also includes assessing the accounting principles used and significant estimates made by management, as well as evaluating the overall financial statement presentation. We believe that our audit provides a reasonable basis for our opinion.

In our opinion, the financial statements referred to above present fairly, in all material respects, the financial position of X Company at December 31, 19X1, and the results of its operations and its cash flows for the year then ended in conformity with generally accepted accounting principles.

This new report form was designed to increase public

awareness of the nature and limitations of the audit. As stated in the first paragraph of the report, management (not the auditors) is primarily responsible for the financial statements.

The second paragraph of the audit report describes just what an audit is. The auditor tests the accounting records and supporting documents to form an opinion on the reasonableness of the financial statements. Standards developed by the American Institute of Certified Public Accountants (AICPA) offer guidance and define the auditor's responsibilities in various situations. For instance, the standards require that the auditor confirm receivables and payables. In order to do this the auditor draws only test samples of these items.

The third paragraph of the audit report contains the auditors' opinion. Auditors may express a "clean," "qualified," or "adverse" opinion, or they may "disclaim" and express no opinion at all. The standard report form quoted above expresses a clean opinion. Based on their tests, the auditors believe the financial statements are "fair" presentations of the company's financial position and earnings for the year.

The auditors also state that the financial statements are "in conformity with generally accepted accounting principles" (GAAP), the accounting profession's collection of rules and basic principles governing financial statement presentation and measurement.(See Key 5.)

A qualified opinion takes exception to "fair presentation" and points out the particular area(s) that the auditors do not believe to be "fair presentation." It is implicit that the auditors believe the remainder of the statements to be fairly presented.

An adverse opinion states that the auditors do not believe the financial statements are "fairly presented." When the auditors issue such an opinion, they will list the factors that led them to this opinion.

Red Flag. The auditors base their opinion of the financial statements on the evidence they gather from the test samples. Because this is far from a complete test of the accounting records, material misstatement may exist without the auditors being aware of it.

10

COMPILATION AND REVIEW REPORTS

Occasionally you may run across a set of financial statements that have been *reviewed* or *compiled*. These types of services are performed by a CPA but do not carry the same weight as an audit, which results in the CPA's issuing an opinion on the fairness of financial statement presentation, as described in Key 9. Because of time and cost considerations, quarterly financial statements are reviewed rather than audited. Businesses that do not regularly make their financial statements available to the public may prefer reviews or compilations to the audit because of cost considerations.

Reviews. A review consists of asking questions of management about the preparation of the financial statements as well as analyzing past and present financial statements to determine if unusual relationships exist. For instance, suppose that for the past several years accounts receivable have averaged $2 million. This year, however, accounts receivable are reported at $4 million. What is the cause of the unexpected relationship? Have the sales been recorded twice? Where relationships appear normal the CPA does not investigate further.

The following examples of differences in audit procedures and review procedures should help you to understand the basic difference between them. In an audit, a CPA would be present at the counting of year-end inventories. In a review, the CPA would merely ask questions about the procedures used to count inventories. Auditing standards require the CPA to obtain written confirmations from customers of the amounts they owe the company in order to evaluate accounts receivable. Written confirmations are also obtained from suppliers indicating the amounts owed by the business, in order to evaluate accounts payable. The CPA would not perform such procedures in a review, but would only ask: Have all sales and payments from customers been recorded? Have all purchases and payments to suppliers been recorded?

In a review report, CPAs must state that they are not aware of any material changes needed to make the financial statements conform to Generally Accepted Accounting Principles (GAAP). CPAs also must state that they have not audited the financial statements and are not expressing an opinion on their fairness of presentation.

Compilations. In a compilation the CPA reads the financial statements and decides whether they are in proper form and appear to contain appropriate disclosures. The CPA also checks the mathematics of the statements. For instance, in examining the balance sheet: Do assets equal liabilities plus owners' equity? CPAs are not required to analyze relationships or to ask management questions about the preparation of the statements. But their reports must state that they have not audited the financial statements and are not expressing an opinion on fairness of presentation.

11

SEC FORMS 10-K, 10-Q, AND 8-K

Part of the job of the Securities and Exchange Commission (SEC) is to ensure that current and potential investors and creditors have equal access to information about companies whose securities are publicly traded. The SEC accomplishes this task by requiring publicly held companies to file information periodically.

The SEC determines what information should be filed and how it should be presented, in addition to acting as a kind of clearing-house for the reports. The major SEC-required forms are the 10-K (annual), 10-Q (quarterly), and 8-K (for significant changes). Although this information is on file at SEC offices, requests for annual or other reports or Form 10-K should be addressed to the treasurers of the individual companies.

Form 10-K. This form must be filed with the SEC annually by publicly traded companies. The filing deadline is 90 days after the close of the company's fiscal year. Form 10-K contains essentially the same information that companies include in their annual reports, but in more detail. Additional information is also required to complete the 10-K. Sometimes a company will issue a combined annual report and 10-K. This is allowed under the SEC's integrated disclosure rules.

The 10-K is divided into four parts, and each part is subdivided into individual items. Where information has been provided elsewhere, the company may reference those sources rather than duplicating the information.

Form 10-K: Contents
Part 1

1. Description of the company's business, including information on different segments of the company (for example, product-lines, industries, domestic and foreign operations, or major classes of customers).
2. Description of the company's property.
3. Description of the legal proceedings in which the company is involved.
4. Discussion of matters that have been voted on by the shareholders.

Part 2

5. Description of the market for the company's common stock including disclosures of: the principal U.S. markets on which the company's common stock is traded, quarterly high and low stock prices for the last two years, approximate number of shareholders, amount and frequency of cash dividends paid in the last two years, and any restrictions on the company's ability to pay dividends.
6. Five-year summary of selected financial data, including net sales (operating revenues), income or loss from continuing operations, income or loss from continuing operations per common share, total assets, long-term debt and redeemable preferred stock, and cash dividends per common share.
7. Management's discussion of the company's financial condition, changes that have occurred in financial condition, and results of operations. This discussion will include management's analysis of the company's liquidity, resources, and operations, the impact of inflation, the cause of major changes in the financial statements that have occurred during the year, and any material contingencies.
8. Financial statements, supplementary data, and auditor's report.

9. Changes in accounting principles and disagreements with the company's auditors.

Part 3

10. List of directors and executive officers.
11. Compensation of the executive officers.
12. Company securities owned by management and major stockholders.
13. Information on related-party transactions, including transactions between the company and management, its subsidiaries, and major stockholders.

Part 4

14. Exhibits, financial statement schedules, reports on Form 8-K.

Form 10-Q. This form is filed by a publicly traded company with the SEC at the end of each of its first three quarters of the fiscal year. The filing deadline is 45 days after the end of the quarter. Form 10-Q contains only quarterly information. The quarterly financial statements contained in the 10-Q have not been audited, only reviewed by the company's CPAs (see Key 10).

Form 8-K. This form is used to report any significant changes that have occurred in the information the company has filed with the SEC. Form 8-K does not contain audited data. Filing of the 8-K must take place within 15 days of any significant change. Some of the changes reported on Form 8-K are changes in the company's controlling interest, major purchases or sales of assets, filing for bankruptcy or receivership, a change of the company's auditors, and resignations of directors.

12

COMPONENTS OF THE BALANCE SHEET

Accountants use a system of record keeping called double-entry bookkeeping. This system is based on the relationship between business resources and the source of those resources. Business resources are called assets and may be obtained either by borrowing (a liability) or by investment by the owners (equity). The relationship between assets, liabilities, and owners' equity can be expressed as:

$$\text{Assets} = \text{Liabilities} + \text{Owners' Equity}$$

If $10,000 of resources are contributed by investors, both assets and equity will be increased by the same amount, $10,000. If $5,000 cash is borrowed from the bank, both assets and liabilities will be increased by $5,000. Thus, after each transaction is recorded, assets will still equal liabilities plus owners' equity.

A balance sheet is a report that displays the assets, liabilities, and owners' equity of a business as of a specific date. The recorded value of the assets will equal the recorded value of the liabilities plus owners' equity. An alternative name for the balance sheet is Statement of Financial Position.

Assets. Those things of value that the business possesses and can use as it attempts to produce a profit are called assets. In order for a company to record an asset on its balance sheet, the resource must possess three characteristics: (1) positive potential cash flow, (2) the ability to be controlled, and (3) the right of use or control, granted in a past transaction or event.

The first characteristic, positive potential cash flow, means that management believes that the resource is capable of bringing more cash into the business than will flow out of the business as the result of using the resource. The purchase of a fleet of delivery trucks, for example, will enable a company to deliver more of its own products to customers in less time, thus increasing its sales. The second characteristic, control, indicates that the resource provides a competitive advantage that can be used as the company sees fit. With the trucks, the company can control its own delivery schedules. The third characteristic reflects the historical nature of accounting. Financial statements only report the results of past transactions or events. Thus, the trucks are first recorded as assets in the period when they were purchased.

In order to be listed as an asset on the balance sheet, a resource must not only possess these three characteristics but must also be capable of being valued. Significant resources often go unrecorded. For instance, employees are the most important resource many businesses have. But, how do you measure and objectively value an employee? You can't! Even though an employee could be considered an asset, valuation problems will prevent them from being listed as such.

Legal ownership is not a required characteristic of an asset. Equipment leased on a long-term lease that transfers the basic rights and risks of ownership will be recorded as an asset on the books of the company leasing the equipment (see Key 7).

Liabilities. The debts of the business—the amounts owed to nonowners—are its liabilities. These possess three major characteristics: (1) they represent the possibility of a future payment of cash to settle the obligation, (2) management has little chance of avoiding the obligation, and (3) the obligation arose in a past transaction or event.

Obligations do not have to be legally binding before they are recorded as a liability on the balance sheet. As noted previously, a pledge to United Way is not legally binding on management, but it will be recorded as a liability. Why? All three characteristics of a liability are present, and the obligation can be valued. The obligation exists as a result of management signing a pledge card (a past transaction or event). There exists the possibility of a future payment of cash to settle the pledge. And to avoid payment would damage the business's reputation.

Owners' Equity. Also called shareholders' equity, owners' equity in a corporation is the difference between the recorded values of the assets and of the liabilities. It includes amounts directly invested by the owners (contributed capital) plus any profits earned by the business that have not been paid out to the owners (retained earnings).

When a company realizes net income, the inflow of assets from revenues has exceeded the outflow of assets to produce those earnings. Since assets have increased and liabilities have not been affected, ownership must have increased. Retained earnings have thus grown.

A simple example will illustrate: Johnson invests $100,000 to begin a business. Immediately after his investment Johnson draws up the following balance sheet.

ASSETS		LIABILITIES	
Cash	$100,000		$0
		OWNER'S EQUITY	
		Contributed Capital	100,000
	$100,000		$100,000

Johnson pays $10,000 to buy inventory (an asset until it is resold). His balance sheet now appears as follows:

ASSETS		LIABILITIES	
Cash	$90,000		$0
Inventory	10,000	OWNER'S EQUITY	
		Contributed Capital	100,000
	$100,000		$100,000

Johnson then sells merchandise that originally cost him $4,500 (expense) for $6,500 (revenue)—a net income of $2,000. His balance sheet would appear as follows:

ASSETS		LIABILITIES	
Cash	$96,500		$0
Inventory	5,500	OWNER'S EQUITY	
		Contributed Capital	100,000
		Retained Earnings	2,000
	$102,000		$102,000

Classified Balance Sheet. A classified balance sheet will generally contain the following categories:

ASSETS	LIABILITIES
Current Assets	Current Liabilities
Long-term Investments	Long-term Liabilities
Property, Plant and Equipment	
Intangibles	SHAREHOLDERS' EQUITY
Other Assets	Capital Stock
	Additional Paid-in Capital
	Retained Earnings

Within each of these categories there are individual accounts. For example, current assets may include cash, short-term investments, receivables, inventories, and prepaid expenses. The categories and the individual accounts comprising a category will be discussed in the next 15 keys, which are illustrated with the various components of a full classified balance sheet.

Red Flags. The balance sheet is like a still photograph. It only shows resources, obligations, and equity at a point in time, typically the fiscal year-end. And, as you can see from our simple example above, each transaction affects the balance sheet, causing it to change immediately.

Assets and liabilities may go unrecorded because of measurement problems. Where such material information cannot be quantified, however, it will be reported in a note to the financial statements (see Keys 6, 7, and 8).

13

CURRENT ASSETS

Current assets are short-term assets and are listed in a separate category in the balance sheet. Current assets are composed of cash, items that will provide cash, and certain items that will prevent the outflow of cash in the short term. The key to understanding the current assets category of the balance sheet is to examine the accountant's definition of current assets phrase by phrase.

Accountants define *short-term* as one year or one company operating cycle, whichever is greater. Thus, short-term may mean different time periods for different companies, depending on their operating cycles. A company's operating cycle is the length of time required to go "from cash to cash" in operations. To explain, cash is first invested in inventory, either by manufacturing something or by purchasing a product for resale. Next, the inventory is sold, creating an account receivable. Finally, the receivable is collected, and cash is put in the till, thus completing the cycle. The length of time a company's cash is tied up in accounts receivable and inventory can be estimated using the technique explained in Key 45/ACTIVITY RATIOS.

Usually, cash is tied up 30 to 60 days in both accounts receivable and in inventories, and a company's operating cycle is anywhere from 60 to 120 days. As a result, the time span for current assets is most often one year. But some companies leave cash in inventories for a very long time. A whiskey distiller, for instance, may age inventory for 12 years during the manufacturing process. The operating cycle for such a distiller may then be the total of the 12 years cash is invested in inventory plus the 30 days cash is invested in receivables! Current assets for such a distillery could thus include items that would provide cash in 12 years and 30 days. This would allow the distiller to include its inventory of aging whisky as a current asset.

The types of assets classified as current assets include:

1. Cash
2. Items that will provide cash in one year or one operating cycle, whichever is greater, including accounts receivable, short-term notes receivable, and inventories of raw materials, supplies, and finished goods
3. Items that prevent the outflow of cash in one year or one operating cycle, whichever is greater, including prepaid insurance, prepaid rent, and employee advances.

A current assets section is shown below.

Cash and temporary cash investments	84.4	89.6
Accounts receivable (less allowance for doubtful accounts: 1987/$5.0 and 1986/$7.6)	400.9	414.1
Contract receivable (Note 3)	94.6	—
Materials, supplies, and fuel stock (at average cost)	97.3	118.4
Inventory	72.9	87.2
Prepayments	21.9	16.0
TOTAL CURRENT ASSETS	772.0	725.3

Red Flags. Sometimes the term working capital is used to refer to current assets. But you must be alert. Working capital is also used to refer to net current assets—or current assets minus current liabilities. Long ago, net working capital was used to refer to net current assets, and working capital referred to current assets, but this distinction is now seldom made.

14

CASH AND RECEIVABLES

Cash. The most active asset in a company's balance sheet is its cash. Few business transactions will occur that do not affect cash in some way, either providing cash or requiring it. Cash itself is a relatively unproductive asset (earning at best a nominal interest rate on time deposits), but it is vitally important to the day-to-day operations of a business. Cash is also the most universally desirable asset that a company possesses: it is easily transported, hard to recognize once off the company premises, and easily convertible into other goods. Cash is subject to more accounting and management controls than any other asset.

Cash includes only the most liquid current assets. To be reported as "cash," an item must be readily available for payment of current obligations. Items classified as cash include:

- coin and currency on hand
- petty cash funds
- checking accounts (unrestricted funds available on deposit in a bank)
- change funds (for cash registers, etc.)

- negotiable instruments (such as personal checks, travelers' checks, cashiers' checks, bank drafts, and money orders.)

Cash balances earmarked for some special purpose should not be reported as "cash." Examples of special-purpose cash balances include bond sinking funds or employee travel funds. Neither are readily available to meet current obligations. Special purpose cash balances are reported in the balance sheet as "restricted funds." Similarly, certificates of deposit, money market funds, Treasury bills, and commercial paper are not readily available to meet current obligations. Still, these items are generally classified and reported as cash equivalents under current assets.

Receivables. All amounts owed to a company that are expected to be settled in cash are called receivables. The chief source of receivables is usually the company's regular trade customers. All receivables can be classified as either trade receivables or nontrade receivables. Trade receivables are mostly accounts or notes receivable. The most common type of receivable reported in the balance sheet, trade receivables also usually represent the largest dollar amount.

Nontrade receivables can be either current or noncurrent. Examples of nontrade receivables are accounts or notes receivable arising from the following types of transaction:

- claims for losses or damages
- claims for tax refunds
- dividends or interest receivable
- advances to employees
- sales of property other than inventory
- deposits with creditors or utilities

Receivables may appear in the current assets section of the balance sheet as illustrated below. Details as to allowances for doubtful accounts, when not shown on the face of the balance sheet, would be in Note One, Significant Accounting Policies.

Sample notes on cash and accounts receivable are shown below.

Note 8: Cash and Marketable Securities

(Millions of dollars)	1987	1986
Cash	$ 9	$ 8
Time deposits	95	34
Certificates of deposit	65	132
Marketable securities	51	72
Total	$ 220	$ 246

The marketable securities are stated at cost, which approximates market value.

Note 9: Accounts Receivable, Net

(Millions of dollars)	1987	1986
Customers	$ 315	$ 289
Unconsolidated subsidiaries and affiliates	16	10
Employee	4	3
Other	28	23
	363	325
Less allowance for losses	7	7
Total	$ 356	$ 318

Red Flags. Certain credit transactions may require the pledging or assignment of receivables as security for a loan. With a "general assignment," all accounts receivable serve as collateral. With a "specific assignment," specific accounts receivable may be pledged as collateral.

Notes receivable may be "discounted" to a bank. When notes receivable are discounted, the company receives immediate cash and the bank receives repayment when the note is collected. When notes receivable are discounted with recourse, the company will disclose any obligations on the discounted notes.

15

INVENTORIES

There are several different types of inventory. For instance, a manufacturer may have inventories of raw materials, inventories of partially completed work in process, and inventories of supplies used in operations, in addition to an inventory of manufactured finished goods available for sale. And a retailer's inventory may consist only of purchased finished goods available for sale.

Inventories are current assets, carried in the balance sheet either at original historical cost, or at the lower of cost or market value. The cost of purchased goods in a retailer's inventory includes the cost of transportation or freight in, but is reduced by any purchase discounts taken by the buyer, any returns made, or any allowances received. A schedule of ending inventories for a retailer is illustrated below.

SCHEDULE OF ENDING INVENTORIES

Beginning Inventory		75,000
Purchases	250,000	
Plus: Freight-in	10,000	
Less: Purchase Discounts	(5,000)	
Returns and Allowances	(15,000)	
Net delivered cost of purchases		240,000

Total goods available for sale	315,000
Less: Cost of goods sold	255,000
Ending inventory	60,000

The components of a manufacturer's inventories will be shown either in the body of the financial statements or in the statement notes. A schedule of inventory components for a manufacturer is illustrated below.

Note B—Inventories
Inventories are valued at cost not in excess of market, using the first-in, first-out (FIFO) method. The major components of inventory as of November 30 were as follows:

(in thousands)	1987	1986
Raw materials	$49,751	$19,753
Work in-process	4,662	2,945
Finished goods	20,254	11,713
	$74,667	$34,411

Since companies acquire inventories at different prices during the year, it is important to know the basis for inventory valuation. The method of inventory valuation is given in Note One of an annual report. The way inventories are valued affects both cost of goods sold and ending inventory; see Key 32/COST OF GOODS SOLD AND INVENTORIES.

Regardless of the inventory valuation method, inventories are usually shown on the balance sheet at the lower of historical cost or current market value. This prevents a company from carrying inventories at an inflated asset amount and forces a company to charge any loss in value against earnings in the period when the loss occurred. Without the lower-of-cost-or-market rule, inventories could be carried as current assets with an inflated value, and the loss (in value) would not be charged against earnings until the goods were sold, possibly in the year following the actual decline in inventory replacement prices. In most cases, managers would have an incentive to delay expensing the lost inventory value, in hopes market prices would rise again in the next year.

Finished-goods inventory turnover and days in inventory are discussed in Key 45/ACTIVITY RATIOS. The turnover of both raw-material and work-in-process inventories can also be calculated, although some of the figures needed may not be available in the company's annual report. There are four important formulas used in calculating turnover for all inventory components, as follows:

$$\text{Finished Goods Turnover} = \frac{\text{Cost of Goods Sold}}{\text{Average Finished Goods Inventory}}$$

$$\text{Work in Process Turnover} = \frac{\text{Cost of Goods Manufactured}}{\text{Average Work in Process Inventory}}$$

$$\text{Raw Material Turnover} = \frac{\text{Raw Material Used}}{\text{Average Raw Material Inventory}}$$

$$\text{Operating Supplies Turnover} = \frac{\text{Operating Supplies Used}}{\text{Average Operating Supplies Inventory}}$$

16

PROPERTY, PLANT AND EQUIPMENT

The category of assets generally listed after Current Assets in the balance sheet is Property, Plant and Equipment. These are the company's long-lived productive assets—including land, buildings, furniture and fixtures, and machinery—and are carried at their historical cost less applicable depreciation, depletion, or amortization (see Key 17/DEPRECIATION and Key 19/DEPLETION AND AMORTIZATION). A note listing buildings, machinery, and equipment is shown on the next page.

The historical cost of a productive asset is the total cost connected with acquiring the asset and readying it for use. For example, the historical cost of a piece of machinery would include its invoice price, delivery charges, installation costs, and the cost of trial production runs to adjust the machine to the desired product quality. In other words, all costs incurred until the time production begins would generally be considered part of the machine's historical cost. Historical cost may also include interest cost on funds borrowed to finance the construction of plant and equipment.

The Property, Plant and Equipment line also generally in-

9. Buildings, machinery, and equipment at December 31, by major classification, were as follows:

	1987	1986	1985
Buildings	$ 2,076	$ 2,071	$ 2,068
Machinery	2,974	3,209	3,284
Patterns, dies, jigs, etc	487	496	448
Furniture and fixtures	300	232	191
Transportation equipment . . .	16	13	14
Construction-in-process	300	167	126
	6,153	6,188	6,131
Less acc. deprec..	3,785	3,852	3,581
Buildings, machinery, and equipment —net	$ 2,368	$ 2,336	$ 2,550

The company had commitments for the purchase or construction of capital assets of approximately $330 at December 31, 1987. Capital expenditure plans are subject to continuous monitoring and changes in such plans could reduce the amount committed.

cludes the assets Leasehold Improvements and Property Subject to Capital Leases. The former is the cost of improvements made to leased property that will revert to its owner at the end of the lease term; the latter is property that has been acquired through a long-term leasing arrangement, which is essentially an alternative purchase and mortgage arrangement (see Key 7/LEASES).

Red Flags. Valuing at historical cost causes problems in that it limits the usefulness of the figures obtained. Historical cost is an objective measure, but it may not be relevant to the decision maker. For instance, a piece of land valued at its 1940 historical cost of $1 million on a balance sheet tells us little about its current worth in terms of sales value or loan value. Comparisons between entities are also hampered by the use of historical cost—comparing the cost of property purchased in 1940 to the cost of similar property in 1988 is misleading. Although the 1988 property has a higher historical cost, it may not be any more productive than the 1940 property.

17

DEPRECIATION

The key to understanding depreciation is to realize what accountants mean by the term. In ordinary usage, depreciation means decline in value. To the accountant, however, depreciation is the assignment of historical cost of a long-lived productive asset to production periods—the matching of costs of production (expenses) with the results of production (revenues). (Review the accrual concept as explained in Key 5, in particular the matching concept.) Rather than recording decline in value as depreciation, the accountant is recording the using-up of the original cost of the asset over its productive life.

The exception to the concept of depreciation is land, which is not used up. Land is a renewable resource. Therefore, land is not depreciated and is valued on the balance sheet at its historical cost.

Companies generally use one (or a combination) of four primary depreciation methods in preparing their annual reports. These methods are (1) straight-line, (2) units of production, (3) sum-of-the-years' digits, and (4) double-declining balance. The depreciation methods used by a company will be disclosed in note 1, as shown below.

Depreciation and Amortization—Prior to July 1, 1986, substantially all of the Company's flight equipment was being depreciated on a straight-line basis to residual values (10% of cost) over a ten-year period from dates placed in service. As a result of a comprehensive review of its fleet plan, effective July 1, 1986, the Company increased the estimated useful lives of substantially all of its flight equipment. Flight equipment that was not already fully depreciated is now depreciated on a straight-line basis to residual values (10% of cost) over a 15-year period from dates placed in service. The effect of this change was a $130 million decrease in depreciation expense, and a $69 million ($1.54 per share) increase in net income, for the year ended June 30, 1987. Ground property and equipment are depreciated on a straight-line basis over their estimated service lives, which range from three to 30 years.

Straight-line depreciation assumes that equal benefit is derived from using the productive asset each year of its useful life. The formula for straight-line depreciation is:

Cost – salvage value/years of useful life = 1 year's depreciation

For example, if a company purchased a machine for $10,000 and at the time of purchase estimated its productive life to be three years, after which it would have a salvage value of $1,000, depreciation expense would be $3,000 per year ($10,000 – $1,000) / 3.

Units-of-production depreciation assumes that revenue produced parallels units of product produced. In other words, in years in which more product is produced the company has greater revenue producing ability. The formula for units-of-production depreciation is:

Cost – salvage value / units of product that can be produced over the life of the asset = per-unit depreciation

To find a year's depreciation expense we would multiply the number of units produced during the year by the per-unit depreciation rate. For example, assuming a cost of $10,000, a salvage value of $1,000, a useful life of three years, and an estimated production of 4 million units of product over the three-year period, the depreciation rate per unit of product produced is [$10,000 – 1,000] / 4,000,000 = $ .00225 per unit. If 1 million units are produced during the year, depreciation expense of $2,250 would be recorded for the year (1,000,000

× .00225).

Declining Balance Methods. Both the sum of the years' digits and double-declining balance are declining balance methods of depreciation. They take more depreciation in the earlier years of an asset's life than in the later years. These methods assume that an asset is most productive (therefore, has the most revenue producing ability) in the early years of the asset's life before wear and tear begin to take their toll.

The formula for the sum of the year's digits is:

Cost – salvage value × years in reverse order / sum-of-the-year's digits.

For a machine that has a $10,000 cost, $1,000 salvage value, and a three year life expectancy, the first year's depreciation expense would be calculated as follows: $10,000 – $1,000 × 3 / (1 + 2 + 3) = $9,000 × 3/6 = $4,500. The second year's depreciation expense would be ($9,000 × 2/6) = $3,000. The final year's depreciation would be ($9,000 × 1/6) = $1,500. Notice that the rate of depreciation is declining year to year (1/2—1/3—1/6), not the depreciation base, which remains $9,000.

The formula for double-declining balance depreciation is net book value of the depreciable asset × (2 / number of years estimated life)

Net book value of the depreciable asset—its original cost minus all depreciation taken to date (*accumulated depreciation*). Using our example of an asset that cost $10,000, with $1,000 salvage value and a three-year estimated life, the first year's depreciation expense would be calculated as: ($10,000 – $0) × 2/3 = $6,667. The second year's depreciation expense would be ($10,000 – $6,667) × 2/3 = $2,222.

The company will actually record only $111 of depreciation in the third and final year of the asset's life. This is the difference between net book value at the beginning of the third year and the estimated salvage value at the end of the third year ($10,000 – $8,889) – $1,000. The double-declining balance method is the only one of the four primary depreciation methods that ignores estimated salvage value in its formula. Therefore, in the final year of the asset's life, the asset must only be depreciated to a net book value equal to its expected salvage value.

Red Flags. The basis for long-lived asset valuation is historical cost. Because depreciation does not measure actual decline in value, the net book value of a long-lived asset (historical cost – accumulated depreciation) is not a good measure of the cost of replacing the asset. Neither is net book value a good measure of what the asset would bring if sold. Long-lived assets with net book value equal to their estimated salvage value—or zero if there is no salvage value—may continue to be used by the company to earn revenue while they are minimally valued on the balance sheet.

Depreciation computations are based largely on estimates of both useful life and salvage value. Should either of these estimates change during the life of the depreciable asset, the company will recompute depreciation from that point forward. This computation will use the net book value as the historical cost and the new estimates of salvage and remaining years of useful life. For example, suppose that management decides at the beginning of the third year that an asset that cost $10,000 and had a $1,000 salvage value and a three-year estimated useful life now has a remaining useful life of three years with a new estimated salvage value of $1,500. Straight-line depreciation expense for that third year would be computed as follows: $10,000 – $6,000 = $4,000, the net book value after two years of straight-line depreciation, then ($4,000 – $1,500)/3 years remaining life = $833 depreciation expense per year.

Comparability is hindered by using different depreciation methods. In our examples, the first year's depreciation expense was: straight-line—$3,000, units of production—$2,250, sum-of-the-years' digits—$4,500, and double-declining balance—$6,667. If four identical companies each used a different one of these depreciation methods to compute depreciation for an identical asset, their net book values of the asset and their net incomes would be different. In other words, choice of depreciation methods can create artificial differences between companies.

18

INTANGIBLES AND OTHER ASSETS

Intangible assets are long-lived productive assets that do not have a physical existence. For the most part, they are legal rights given to the company that offer it a competitive edge and aid it in producing revenue. Examples of intangible assets include patents, copyrights, trademarks and tradenames, franchises, organization costs, and purchased goodwill.

Initially, intangible assets are recorded at historical cost. As this historical cost is written off against production periods (see Key 19/AMORTIZATION), the recorded value of the intangible will decline.

There are six major types of intangible assets along with a catchall category, Other Assets.

Patents. A patent is an exclusive right to use, manufacture, or sell a product or process. In the United States, patents are granted for 17 years. The patent's historical cost will be expensed against the revenues it helps produce over the lesser of its legal life or its estimated economic life. In fields where technology is rapidly changing (such as computer hardware and software) a patent's economic life may be less than its legal life.

Copyrights. A copyright gives exclusive control to the creator of a literary, musical, or artistic work. Copyrights may be assigned or sold. Currently, copyrights are granted for the life of the creator plus 50 years. However, a copyright's historical cost will be expensed over the lesser of its estimated economic life or 40 years. (Accounting principles require that intangibles be expensed over a period that may not exceed 40 years.) The historical costs of literary and musical copyrights are frequently expensed over the life of the first printing.

Trademarks and tradenames. These symbols or words serve to identify a product or company. They are initially granted for 20 years and are subject to indefinite renewals. Theoretically, then, they have unlimited lives. Their historical cost will be expensed over the lesser of their estimated economic life or 40 years.

Franchises and Organizational Costs. A *franchise* is the right to sell a product or service under a tradename. The cost of the franchise will be expensed over the life of the franchise with, again, a limit of 40 years. *Organizational costs* are the initial costs of creating a business entity. They include attorneys' fees and other fees. These costs will also be expensed over a period of not more than 40 years.

Purchased Goodwill. When one business purchases another, it may be willing to pay more for that business than the market value of the net assets. (Net assets represent the difference between the value of a company's total assets and its total liabilities.) To an accountant this "excess of cost over the market value" is goodwill. Why might a company be willing to pay more than market value for the net assets of another company? The reason is generally that the purchaser is also acquiring intangibles—the reputation of the products or service of the purchased company, its personnel's potential, monopoly position, etc.

Accounting principles allow only purchased goodwill to be recorded in the accounts (internal development of a business reputation may not be assigned a value and recorded). Although goodwill may have an indefinite economic life, it must be amortized over a period not to exceed 40 years.

51

Research and Development Costs. These are the costs of discovering new technology and applying it to products, process, or services. Occasionally, research and development costs will be recorded as assets and amortized over the lesser of their economic life or 40 years. However, accounting principles require that the majority of research and development costs be expensed as they arise. This is owing to the uncertainty of future benefits. In fact, most research and development projects do not result in a marketable product, process, or service.

The total cost of research and development for the fiscal period must be disclosed. While the majority of projects may not succeed, they keep a company competitive. The proportion of dollars spent on R & D to a company's sales is one measure of management's investment in the future.

Other Assets. This catchall category includes business resources that cannot be classified as current assets, investments, property, plant, equipment, or intangibles. It may include long-lived assets awaiting sale and no longer being used in production. Classifying such assets under Property, Plant and Equipment would imply they are currently in use. Prepayments of expenses (such as a three-year insurance policy) may also be classified as "other." A note on intangible assets is shown below.

Note 15: *Intangible assets are recorded at cost less amortization.*

	Estimated Remaining Life*	1987	1986
Patents	6	$ 1,057	$1,234
Goodwill	35	639	653
Other intangible assets	25	257	257
Total		$ 1,953	$2,144

*Weighted average, in years, at December 31, 1987.

19

DEPLETION AND AMORTIZATION

The key to understanding *depletion* and *amortization* is to understand how accountants use the terms. Depletion and amortization (like depreciation) represent the assignment of historical cost of a long-lived asset to production periods— the matching of the costs of production (expenses) with production's results (revenues). This cost assignment is called *depletion* for natural resources and *amortization* for intangible assets.

The method of depletion most often used is a units-of-production formula:

Cost of the natural resource / estimated recoverable (removable) units of the resource = per unit depletion rate

If a stand of timber cost us $2 million and we estimate that it will produce 4 million cords, our depletion rate is $ .50 per cord ($2 million / 4 million). If we remove 500,000 cords in one year, our depletion expense for that year would be 500,000 × $.50) = $250,000.

Amortization is recorded on a straight-line basis (cost / number of amortization periods). The amortization period is the lesser of the intangible's economic life, legal life, or 40 years. Suppose we develop a patented process to use in the production of our product. The research and development costs were $15 million and were expensed throughout the research and development phase (see Key 18/INTANGIBLES, Research and Development). Attorneys' fees and patent application costs totaled $500,000 (the amount recorded as the historical cost of the patent). We estimate that the patented process will have an economic life of 12 years, so we will expense this patent over the 12-year period rather than its legal life of 17 years. Amortization expense will be ($500,000 / 12) = $41,667 per year.

Amortization is also taken on "Leasehold Improvements" and "Property Subject to Capital Leases" (see Key 16/PROPERTY, PLANT AND EQUIPMENT). If leased property will be returned to the lessor at the end of the lease term, the recorded cost of improvements to the leased property will be expensed over the term of the lease. If the company will keep the property after the expiration of the lease, it should expense the improvements and property over their economic lives. In this case, the method of computing amortization should be the method we use to depreciate similar assets that we own.

Red Flags. Just as is the case with depreciation, the net book values of natural resources and intangibles are not good measures of either the cost of replacing these assets or the amount that could be received if they were sold. Depletion and amortization computations are based only on estimates, which are of course subject to change. When an estimate changes, the net book value of the asset at that time becomes the basis for depletion or amortization over the remaining units of the natural resource or amortization period. Management's ability to choose an arbitrary amortization period for certain intangibles like purchased goodwill (as long as the period does not exceed 40 years) may create artificial differences between companies and may lessen comparability.

ing shares of CDE Corporation for $2 million. This investment represents one third of the outstanding shares. CDE's owners' equity has a recorded value of $6 million. Our investment account will reflect one third of CDE's owners' equity, or:

Investment $2,000,000 | CDE's Owner's Equity $6,000,000

If CDE has net income of $900,000 for the year, our investment will increase $300,000, or:

Initial			
Investment	$2,000,000	CDE's Owner's Equity	$6,000,000
+ Income	300,000	+ Income	900,000
	$2,300,000		$6,900,000

Next, CDE pays $450,000 in dividends; we receive $150,000. The dividends are a withdrawal of investment and will reduce our investment account, or:

Initial			
Investment	$2,000,000	CDE's Owner's Equity	$6,000,000
+ Income	300,000	+ Income	900,000
–Dividends	(150,000)	–Dividends	(450,000)
	$2,150,000		$6,450,000

Notice that each time CDE's equity increases or decreases, our investment increases or decreases proportionately. Because we own one third of CDE, our investment is recorded at one third of the value of CDE's owners' equity. If we had paid more than $2 million for our investment in CDE, the excess amount paid would be considered goodwill (see Key 18). Accounting rules require that goodwill be expensed over a period of 40 years or less. As this occurs, the value of our market value is less than their cost, we believe that a loss is likely to occur. Our best estimate of that loss is the difference between the investments' current market value and their historical cost.

If the investments are long-term, the unrealized loss is no longer "likely to occur." Thus, we will merely reduce the investment portfolio to its current market value and deduct from owners' equity the Net Unrealized Loss on Noncurrent Marketable Equity Securities.

When we prepare the next balance sheet, if the investments' cost are less than their current market value, they will be written back up only to cost. Any profit (amount by which market value exceeds cost) is recorded only at the actual time of sale. If the portfolio is short-term, we will record the difference on the income statement as revenue or gain. If the portfolio is long-term, we will increase the investment account back only to cost and remove the negative owners' equity account Net Unrealized Loss on Noncurrent Marketable Equity Securities.

Equity Method. When investors can exercise significant influence over the affairs of the company in which they have invested, the equity method of accounting is used. If an investor owns, say, 20% of the outstanding voting shares in a corporation, he may be able to elect 20% of the directors. Accountants assume that significant influence exists once an investor acquires 20% or more of a company's common stock.

An accountant using the equity method initially records the investment at historical cost. As the company (the investee) earns income, the investors record their share as income from investment. This will increase the value of their investment. But as dividends are paid to them, they reduce the value of their investment because dividends are assumed to be a return of prior earnings, a withdrawal of investment. Recording income and dividends in this manner causes the investment account to mirror the changes that are occurring in the investee's owner's equity.

For example, assume that we buy 10,000 of the outstand-

Type of Investment	Balance Sheet Valuation Method	
	Short-term	*Long-term*
Common Stock	Lower of Cost or Market	Varies*
Preferred Stock	Cost	Cost
Bonds	Cost	Present Value

*If company owns < 20% of outstanding shares: Lower of Cost or Market. If company owns > 20% but < 50% of outstanding shares: Equity Method. If company owns > 50% of outstanding shares: parent-subsidiary relationship, requiring consolidated financial statements (see Key 40).

Cost Method. When an accountant uses the cost method of valuation, the investment is recorded on the balance sheet value at its historical cost. Income from the investment is recorded when dividends are declared or interest is due.

Lower-of-Cost-or-Market Method. When an accountant uses the lower-of-cost-or-market-method, the investment is recorded on the balance sheet at its historical cost unless its current market value is less. Income from the investment is recorded when dividends are declared.

Suppose we own two stocks, UVW, Inc. and XYZ, Ltd. The cost of UVW was $100 per share, of XYZ $200 per share. At the end of the fiscal year UVW is selling for $110 per share, XYZ for $160 per share. We would group these stocks together into a portfolio consisting of all investments in common stock where the company owns less than 20% of the outstanding shares. We would then compare the cost of these shares to their current market values. In our case the portfolio cost is $300 ($100 + $200) and the current market value is $270 ($110 + $160). Because the current market value of our portfolio is $30 less than its historical cost ($300 − $270), we will write it down in value $30 and report it on the balance sheet at $270. The write-down is called an *unrealized loss*.

If the investments are short-term, the unrealized loss will be recorded in the income statement as expense or loss. This is the conservative approach. We are accounting for these investments as a contingency (see Key 7). Because we plan to hold these investments a short time (less than a year) and their investment will decrease. After all of the goodwill has been expensed, our investment account will reflect our portion of the investee's recorded owners' equity.

Present Value. Long-term investments in bonds are recorded at present value. The present value of a bond is its cash value at a point in time. Suppose we can buy a ten-year, $1,000 bond that pays 10% interest annually for $950. We will record our investment at $950. If we hold the bond until it matures we will receive a total of $1,050 more than we originally invested. Each year, for ten years, we will receive $100 of interest income. The additional $50 (the discount) is earned by holding the bond. (We will receive $1,000 at maturity, but we only invested $950.) Each year we record part of the $50 as being earned. One way to record this is to assume that the discount is earned equally during the holding period (straight-line amortization). In this case we would earn in $5 of the discount each year. Each year as we record the discount as being earned, the investment will be increased in value $5 and interest income will be reported as $105 ($100 plus $5 of discount earned). By maturity the investment must have a recorded value of $1,000. That is its cash value at that point in time.

Red Flags. There are many ways to value investments. Be sure you understand how an investment has been valued. Notes to the financial statements may provide estimates of the current market value of the company's investments.

In addition to the general rules we have given you here, special industries have their own valuation methods. For instance, insurance companies and brokerage firms value their short-term investments at current market value even if this is greater than historical cost.

21

CURRENT LIABILITIES

Current liabilities are those obligations of the business that are expected to be paid within one year of the date on the balance sheet. These liabilities include:

Trade Accounts Payable. Amounts owed to suppliers for merchandise or services. For example, an unpaid invoice for merchandise purchases, or the utility bill.

Short-term Notes Payable. Short-term interest-bearing debt. Notes are formal documents showing the amount borrowed (principal) and stating as an annual rate the percentage interest that must be paid. Only the principal is recorded on the balance sheet under the title "Notes Payable." Any interest that the company owes is called interest payable.

Current Portion of Long-term Debt. The portion of principal on long-term debt that will be paid within the year. Long-term debt is usually payable in installments (for example, mortgage payments). Any unpaid interest on long-term debt is recorded as interest payable.

Interest Payable. The unpaid interest on short-term and long-term debt. This is the interest charge for the days from the last payments to the balance sheet date.

Unearned Revenues. When customers pay for products or services in advance, a liability is created. Revenue will not be recorded until the product is delivered to the customer or the service is completed (see Key 5/Revenue Recognition).

Tax and Other Withholdings. Employers are required to withhold income taxes and Social Security taxes (FICA taxes) from employees' paychecks. These withholdings plus additional FICA taxes and unemployment taxes must be paid quarterly.

Income Taxes Payable. The portion of income taxes the business has not yet paid. These are taxes due on the company's earnings (not withholdings as above).

Contingencies. A number of "likely to occur" contingencies are recorded as liabilities (see Key 7). Examples are, "Vacation Wages Payable" and "Estimated Liabilities Under Warranties." "Vacation Wages Payable" is not paid until the employees have taken their vacations. "Estimated Liabilities Under Warranties" is the estimated cost of repairing any defective items manufactured and sold under warranty. Only the portion of the contingencies expected to be paid in the coming year is classified under current liabilities. Be sure to read the notes to the financial statements to get a feel for how significant the contingencies are.

A note relating to current liabilities reported in the balance sheet is shown below.

10. Current liabilities (in thousands)

Trade accounts payable	$30,520	$39,022
Other accounts payable	8,011	9,382
	$38,531	$48,404
Insurance	$14,611	$14,616
Interest	8,934	7,352
Pensions	7,358	9,925
Payroll and vacation pay	7,338	9,920
Taxes other than income taxes	2,268	4,653
Other	21,692	15,914
	$100,732	$110,784

22

NONCURRENT LIABILITIES

Noncurrent (or long-term) liabilities are those obligations of the business that are not expected to be paid for at least one year from the date on the balance sheet. Noncurrent liabilities are carried at their present values. This is the amount of money the company could pay to settle the debt at the balance sheet date. It excludes any future interest, which is not yet due. Most noncurrent liabilities call for periodic payments of principal and interest. The portion of principal that will be due within the year will be classified as a current liability (see Key 21).

Examples of noncurrent liabilities include Long-term Notes and Mortgages Payable, Bonds Payable (see Key 23), Obligations Under Capital Leases (see Key 7), Unfunded Accrued Pension Cost (see Key 8), and Deferred Tax Liability (see Key 37).

Unless you carefully read the notes to the financial statements you will not understand noncurrent liabilities. Many long-term debt covenants place restrictions on the borrower. For instance, a debt covenant may require us to maintain a 2:1 current ratio (the ratio of current assets to current liabilities—see Key 46). What if our current ratio is only 1.9:1? Then we are technically in default on our long-term obligation and it can be called due at any time. Unless management believes the deficiency can be corrected within the specified grace period, the debt will have to be reclassified as current.

Settling Debt Before Maturity. Sometimes a company will pay off debt before it is due. Any settlement of debt before its due date will cause the company to report a gain or loss. The company will have a gain if the cost of settling the debt is less than the debt's recorded value on the balance sheet (including any interest due). The company will have a loss if the cost of settling the debt is greater than the debt's recorded value on the balance sheet (including any interest due). These gains and losses must be reported on the income statement as extraordinary items (see Key 36). Why might a company take a loss to settle a debt before it is due? The loss may be less than the future interest payments, or the company may now be able to borrow money at lower interest rates.

Troubled Debt Restructurings. Sometimes a company experiences problems repaying its debts. A troubled debt restructuring is a situation in which the creditor grants concessions to help the debtor avoid defaulting. The concessions may take the form of the debtor's transferring assets or stock to the creditor, or modifying the terms of debt.

The creditor may agree to settle the debt for noncash assets or stock with a market value less than the recorded value of the debt (including any interest due). In this case the debtor will report a gain on the restructuring equal to the amount by which the debt exceeds the market value of the assets given the creditor. The gain will generally be reported on the debtor's income statement as an extraordinary item.

When the creditor agrees to modify the terms of debt (principal, interest rate, length of time, etc.), the debtor may have to pay more or less than the recorded value of the debt plus any interest due. If the total of the new payments called for is less than the recorded value of the debt (including any interest due), the debtor will record a gain—again, generally reported as an extraordinary item. Payments made by debtors after restructuring are considered to be payments of principal.

These debtors will not recognize interest expense; they could not even pay the debt owed, let alone additional interest.

On the other hand, what if modifying the terms of debt results in total payments that exceed the recorded value of the debt (including any interest due)? In this case the debtor will recognize the recorded value of the debt as the principal of the restructured debt. The amount by which the new payments exceed this principal is the debtor's interest expense over the remaining term of the debt.

A typical schedule of long-term debt, showing interest rates and repayment dates, follows.

Note 7—Long-term debt:

	May 31,	
	1987	1986
	(in thousands)	
8.45% unsecured term loan, due 1993	$25,000	$ —
9.45%–11.7% notes payable, due through 1990	8.354	10,135
8.25% capital equipment purchase agreement payable in installments through 1991	3,386	3,779
8.25%–13.75% capital equipment lease obligations, due through 1991	1,467	2,324
12.5% note payable, secured by certain property, plant and equipment, payments due semi-annually to 1990	1,575	1,826
Other	220	653
Total	40,002	18,717
Less current maturities	4,800	3,417
	$35,202	$15,300

The $25 million term loss agreement requires, among other things, the maintenance of specified financial ratios and balances and contains limits on the amount of investments and sales of assets.

Amounts of long-term debt payable during the five years following May 31, 1987 are summarized as follows:

	Long-Term	Capital Lease Obligations		
	Debt Excluding Capital Lease Obligations	Minimum Lease Payments	Amount Representing Interest	Total
	(in thousands)			
1988	$4,427	$492	$(119)	$4,800
1989	1,354	468	(61)	1,761
1990	6,338	468	(52)	6,754
1991	1,334	291	(22)	1,603
1992	82	2	—	84
Later Years	25,000	—	—	25,000
	$38,535	$1,721	$(254)	$40,002

Red Flags. There is generally no problem understanding the noncurrent liabilities section of the balance sheet, other than the areas cited above (early extinguishment, troubled debt restructuring). Most difficulties arise in interpreting bonds payable, discussed in the next Key. The appropriateness of a company's debt level can be evaluated by comparing a ratio of debt to total assets to the standard industry ratio.

23

BONDS AND AMORTIZATION

When a company needs to borrow a large amount of money—perhaps $20 million—it has two basic choices: It can seek one lender who will supply the entire $20 million or it can seek a series of smaller lenders and obtain the total amount needed in several smaller sums. A company that issues bonds is taking the second option. A typical corporate bond is a debt agreement for $1,000. Thus, a $20 million debt is divided into 20,000 bonds, each for a debt of $1,000.

When an investor (lender) "buys" $50,000 in bonds, the investor has, in essence, agreed to lend the company $50,000. The interest rate, interest payment schedule (usually semiannual), and bond maturity date (when the principal amount is returned) are all contained in the bond. The bond debt may be secured (backed by collateral) or unsecured. Bonds for unsecured debt are called *debentures*. All the bonds may be retired (repaid) at the same time, or they may be structured to mature (come due) in increments. Bonds that mature in increments are called *serial bonds*.

Amortization. A typical bond might be for a debt of $1,000 for ten years, with interest at 10% per year, paid semiannually. The company is, in essence, making two promises: (1) to pay the lender $1,000 in ten years, and (2) to pay interest of $100 ($1,000 \times .10$) each year. As long as the market rate of interest is 10% for bonds of that particular type (secured or unsecured), for the same term and for companies in the same risk class, the company can issue the bond without problem, receiving $1,000.

But, suppose the interest rate rises before the bond is issued. A lender would then no longer purchase a $1,000 bond (and agree to lend $1,000) for 10% interest. The lender would either demand a higher current yield or would insist on investing less than $1,000 in order to receive the payments (principal and interest) described in the bond agreement. Perhaps the lender would agree to lend only $900 in exchange for the payments described in the bond. But the bond issuer would still pay

1. At the end of ten years	$1,000
2. In equal semiannual payments each year (100×10)	$1,000
Total amount paid	$2,000
Less amount received from lender	900
Excess paid over amount received	$1,100

The excess paid over the amount received is the *true cost* of the funds. The company pays $100 cash in interest per year, but the true average annual cost of the money borrowed is $110 ($1,100/10$) per year. The company records the $100 cash outflow each year and the $110 average annual expense. The extra $10 is the amortization of the excess paid over the amount received. (The amortization of bond investments is explained in Key 20.)

When bonds are presented in an annual report, details of the security agreement (if any), the maturity dates, and the interest rates will be in the notes to the financial statements. The bonds are shown under long-term debt in the liabilities section of the financial statements. When a bond is issued at face (for $1,000), the bond will be presented in the balance sheet as follows:

Bond payable (see note x) $1,000

If the market interest rate is more or less than the interest in the bond agreement, the bonds will be sold at a discount or premium, and presentation will be different. If a bond was issued for $900 (as described above), it would appear in the financial statements as follows:

Bond payable (see note x) $1,000
less discount on bonds payable   100   900

Bonds sold for more than face amount are presented in a similar fashion. A bond issued for $1,100 would appear in the financial statments with a premium rather than a discount.

Bonds payable (see note x) $1,000
plus premium on bonds payable   100   1,100

A schedule of bonds payable (debentures), disclosing the interest rates and maturity dates, is shown below.

	1987	1986
5.45% debentures maturing 1984 to 1991, less $5.3 in treasury in 1987 and $6.3 in 1986	$ 2.3	$ 2.3
6% debentures maturing in 1984 to 1992, less 6.1% in treasury in 1987 and $7.2 in 1986	6.1	7.7
7.95% debentures maturing 1985 to 1999, less $2.0 in treasury in 1987 and $3.3 in 1986	72.0	77.3
9.20% debentures maturing 1986 to 2005, less $17.3 in treasury in 1987 and $8.4 in 1986	118.3	134.4
8.55% debentures maturing 1989 to 2008, less $4.3 in treasury in 1987 and $4.2 in 1986	95.7	95.8
11-7/8% debentures maturing 1993 to 2012, less $14.0 in treasury in 1987	86.0	100.0
8-5/8% debentures maturing 1997 to 2016	150.0	150.0
8-1/2% debentures maturing 1998 to 2017	150.0	—
	$ 680.4	$567.5

24

OWNERS' EQUITY

Equity is simply a term meaning "property rights." When the balance sheet components were discussed in Key 12, it was evident that the total assets, or properties, owned by the company belonged to one of two parties—the creditors of the company or its owners. The equity (property rights) of creditors is called debt or liabilities. The equity (property rights) of owners is called owners' equity, stockholders' equity, or (sometimes) capital. The amount of owners' equity can be calculated by subtracting the creditors' equity (liabilities) from the total assets of the company, as: $A - L = OE$. Expressed in this form, owners' equity is sometimes called "net assets," meaning "assets net of (less) liabilities."

The key to understanding owners' equity is to realize that both amounts—liabilities and owners' equity—represent claims of parties against the assets (again, property rights), but the amounts also represent the sources of the assets.

When creditors have transactions with a company, the transactions are commonly described as being "at arm's length." But when owners have transactions with their own company, it is as related parties, not at arm's length. Since owners can legally remove capital as dividends only under certain conditions and only from certain sources, the focus in accounting for owners' equity is on sources of capital.

A complex owners' equity presentation could have capital that came from many sources:

> Donations (see Key 28)
> Treasury stock transactions (see Key 26)
> Preferred stock (see Key 25)
> Subscribed stock (see Key 28)
> Common stock (see Key 25)
> Appropriated retained earnings (see Key 26)
> Unappropriated retained earnings (see Key 26)

A simple owners' equity section from an actual balance sheet is shown below.

Stockholders' Equity		
Preferred stock—cumulative—$1.00 par		
Authorized—10,000,000 shares		
Issued and outstanding—none		
Common stock—$1.00 par value		
Authorized—100,000,000 shares		
Issued—22,048,624 shares in 1987		
and 16,252,655 shares in 1986	22,049	16,253
Additional paid-in capital	154,850	59,667
Retained earnings	60,554	45,848
Foreign currency translation adjustment	938	—
	238,391	121,768
Less 50,289 shares in 1987 and 21,764		
shares in 1986 of common stock in		
treasury—at cost	687	274
	237,704	121,494

For each issue of stock, the number of shares authorized, issued and outstanding and the par or stated value is given. Dividend and call values are included for preferred stocks. The nature of any appropriation of retained earnings is disclosed. Some information about owners' equity will be included in the body of the financial statements. Additional information will be disclosed in the notes.

25

CLASSES OF STOCK

Basically, all stock issued by a company is either preferred stock or common stock, regardless of what name the stock may be given. And, although some companies may describe several different types or classes, there is (except in very rare cases) only one class of common stock. All other classes of stock, regardless of name, are preferred in some way over the one class of common stock.

If a company is liquidated, all creditors are paid proceeds of the liquidation before the claims of stockholders are considered. Among the different classes of stock, there is a ranking as to preference in receiving the proceeds of the liquidation. The stock with the lowest preference as to assets on liquidation is common stock. All other classes of stock are classes of preferred stock, since those stockholders have preference over common stockholders in liquidation and, as will be discussed, perhaps in other ways as well.

By virtue of their bottom ranking as to claims on assets on liquidation, common stockholders are said to be the residual equity holders; they receive any residue left after all creditors and all holders of other classes of stock have been paid. Common stockholders may receive nothing, or they may receive a great deal when a company is liquidated. All creditors and preferred shareholders have a contractually stated amount that they will receive if the company is liquidated and funds are available. Common stockholders have no such contractually stated amount. Thus, common shareholders take the greatest risk but may also receive the greatest reward.

Dividends on preferred stock usually must be paid before dividends on common stock are paid. If the company does not create enough earnings so that the board of directors can declare dividends for both common and preferred shareholders, common shareholders may receive no dividends.

On the other hand, preferred shareholders have no voice in company management. They are, in fact, more like long-term bondholders (creditors) than owners: both receive a fixed payment each year (as dividend or interest), and both have preference over common stockholders as to assets on liquidation, but neither has a vote in company management. The difference is that unless the company has insufficient assets, long-term bondholders will eventually be repaid their investment, and preferred stockholders will not.

To understand preferred stock, there are three additional points we must address.

1. *Dividend calculation.* The dividend rate for preferred stock is a set amount each year. The dividend is usually stated as a dollar amount per share (i.e., a $5 preferred share pays $5 dividends) or as a percentage of par value (i.e., an 8%, $100-par-value preferred share pays $8 dividends). Par value is an arbitrary amount assigned to shares of stock, both common and preferred. *Par value* (and a similar term, *stated value*) had meaning decades ago when securities regulations were different, but have little significance now, other than as a vehicle for calculating dividends on preferred stock or, occasionally, a discount on common stock.

2. *Obligation for missed dividend payments.* If the dividend agreement on preferred stock is *cumulative*, a company must catch up any missed dividend payments to preferred shareholders before dividends can be paid to common shareholders. This is important. A company has no legal obligation

to pay dividends until they are declared by the board of directors. Thus, even though preferred dividends are set, there is no guarantee that they will be paid until they are declared by the board. For example, assume dividends to preferred shareholders would total $100,000 per year, but the company does not declare and does not pay dividends for years 1 and 2. In year 3, the board declares total dividends of $350,000. If preferred dividend payments are cumulative, the distribution schedule is shown below.

For Preferred Stock:

Current year dividend (Year 3)	$100,000
Prior year dividends (Years 1 and 2)	200,000
Total dividends for preferred stockholders	$300,000
Available for dividends to common stockholders	50,000
Total dividends paid	$350,000

A noncumulative distribution of the same $350,000 under the conditions described is shown below.

For Preferred Stock:

Current year dividend (Year 3)	$100,000
Prior year dividend (Years 1 and 2)	0
Total dividends for preferred stockholders	$100,000
Available for dividends to common stockholders	250,000
Total dividends paid	$350,000

3.   *Conversion privilege.* Some preferred stock agreements contain an option allowing the preferred stock to be exchanged for a set number of common shares. To make preferred shares more attractive to investors, the stock may be convertible to common shares in some ratio (10 shares of common for 1 share of preferred, for example).

Common and preferred stock are shown in the financial statement excerpts in Keys 26 and 27.

26

TREASURY STOCK

Stock issued by a company may later be reacquired by the company. In some cases, the company may retire or cancel this stock. When reacquired stock is not retired or canceled, it is referred to as treasury stock.

Treasury stock is not an asset. A company cannot create an asset by holding stock in itself. Although treasury stock, like retired stock, represents a decrease in outstanding stock, the reduction in shares outstanding is not made on the balance sheet. The treasury stock is shown as a reduction in stockholders' equity in one of two ways.

1. The treasury stock may be shown at par value as reduction in common stock.

Stockholders' Equity

Contributed capital:		
Common stock at par	$500,000	
Less treasury stock at par	100,000	
	$400,000	
Paid in capital in excess of par	80,000	$480,000
Retained earnings		200,000
Total stockholders' equity		$680,000

2. The treasury stock may be shown at reacquisition cost as a reduction of total stockholders' equity.

Stockholders' Equity

Contributed Capital:		
Common stock at par	$500,000	
Paid in capital in excess of par	80,000	$580,000
Retained earnings		200,000
Total		780,000
Less treasury stock at cost		100,000
Total stockholders' equity		$680,000

Under either method, total stockholders' equity is decreased by the purchase of treasury shares.

Just as treasury stock is not an asset, a loss or gain cannot result from treasury stock transactions. "Things" happen that you and I would call a "loss" (reacquiring treasury stock for $20 per share and later reissuing it for $12) or a "gain" (reacquiring treasury stock for $30 per share and later reissuing it for $40). But it is illegal for a company to produce a gain or loss transacting in its own stock. When total stockholders' equity is decreased by treasury stock transactions (a loss), the decrease is generally taken directly from retained earnings. No loss is recorded.

When total stockholders' equity is increased by treasury stock transactions (a gain), the increase is recorded as a separate source of capital called Paid-in Capital from Treasury Stock Transactions.

27

RETAINED EARNINGS AND APPROPRIATIONS

When we discussed owner's equity in Key 24, we pointed out that the components of owners' equity represented both property rights and sources of assets. Retained earnings is the dollar amount of assets furnished by earnings of the company that were not distributed as dividends. The key to understanding retained earnings is to realize that such earnings do not represent cash but are only a source of assets.

This logic can be expanded. If a company earns $500,000 and does not declare dividends, retained earnings would be increased by the $500,000 retained in the business. But what does a company do with this $500,000? Management may expand the business (buy new equipment or increase inventories, for instance) or may repay an outstanding loan. The $500,000 increase in retained earnings documents a source of net assets (assets minus liabilities), but does not indicate which assets were provided by the income.

In addition to being a source of assets, total retained earnings is also the maximum amount that can be distributed to stockholders as dividends. The company probably does not have cash available to pay dividends in the amount of retained earnings (nor would the company wish to, if earnings can be reinvested in the business). A company frequently distributes a portion of each year's earnings as dividends in some general pattern, perhaps some amount per share or some percentage of earnings. The remainder is reinvested in the business.

A company that embarks on a special project may limit dividend payments until the project is completed. The company may be required to do this by a major creditor or may simply limit dividend payments in order to preserve cash for expansion. When management limits dividend payments, there are two methods of notifying stockholders: (1) explain the action in the notes to the financial statements, or (2) appropriate a portion of retained earnings.

The portion of retained earnings listed as appropriated in the owners' equity section of the balance sheet is not available for dividend payments. When the project is completed, appropriated retained earnings are unappropriated and again available for dividend payments. Cash may have been spent on the project (building a plant, retiring bonds) and the composition of assets changed, but retained earnings are unaffected except for changing the designation of the appropriated component back to unappropriated. A note discussing appropriated and unappropriated retained earnings is shown below.

7. Retained Earnings.
The provisions of certain of the Company's loan agreements limit the payment of cash dividends under certain circumstances. Retained earnings not restricted under these provisions at December 31, 1987, 1986, and 1985 were $231 million, $202 million and $266 million, respectively.

Red Flags. Companies may use an appropriation of retained earnings simply to reduce the size of unappropriated retained earnings "available" for dividends. Uninformed investors may believe they should receive more of the earnings retained in the business, or labor unions may believe that wages should be higher—neither group realizing that the retained earnings are invested in equipment, in building new plants, or in acquiring more inventory, thus creating the potential for more profit for owners and wages for workers.

28

DONATED CAPITAL AND SUBSCRIBED STOCK

When companies issue stock, they may do so outright, selling stock and receiving cash, property, or services in exchange—or stock may be issued on a subscription basis. A stock subscription is a legally binding contract between the issuing company and the subscriber or purchaser of the stock. Stock subscription agreements allow payment for the stock to be deferred. In these cases, the company has a legal claim for the contract price of the stock, and the purchaser has the legal status of a stockholder (unless specific rights are withheld by state law or contract).

The company's legal claim to the stock contract price is recorded in the balance sheet (generally as a current asset) as "Stock Subscriptions Receivable." Stock subscriptions are like other company receivables: the purchaser/stockholder pays against the outstanding balance according to the contract agreement. The stock certificates are ordinarily not issued until the contract price is paid in full.

When the subscription agreement is signed, the source of this new asset is shown in the owners' equity section of the balance sheet as an increase in two accounts:

1. The par value of the stock is recorded in an account called "Common Stock Subscribed."
2. Any excess over par value is recorded in the account "Premium on Common Stock" or "Paid in Capital in Excess of Par."

When the subscribed stock is fully paid, there will be no subscription receivable carried in current assets and "Common Stock Subscribed" is transferred to "Common Stock."

When property or services are donated to a company, the value of the asset is recorded and the source of the asset is shown as a corresponding increase in owners' equity called "Paid-in Capital from Donations." If the donation is very large, the nature of the donation may be identified, as in "Paid-in Capital from Donated Plant Site."

Red Flags. While a stock subscription agreement is a legal contract and the subscription receivable is a legitimate receivable, corporate policy and state law vary as to how a defaulted subscription is treated. When a subscriber defaults, the company may take any of the following actions:

1. Refund amount received
2. Refund amount received less cost of reselling the stock
3. Declare amount received as forfeited by the subscriber
4. Issue shares equal to the amount already received

29

INCOME STATEMENT COMPONENTS

Annual business income or loss is computed by subtracting the expenses that occurred during the year from the revenues earned during the year. If revenues exceed expenses, the business has earned income. If expenses exceed revenues, a loss has occurred. Revenues and expenses are recorded at the time they are earned or occur regardless of when cash is received or paid. This is the accrual concept, which is used to measure business activity and income (see Key 38/ACCRUAL ACCOUNTING VERSUS CASH FLOW).

The income statement reports the results of business activities for a period of time (typically a fiscal year). These results are classified as revenues and expenses. Revenues measure the inflow of new assets to the business; expenses measure the outflow of assets or the using up of assets in that same process. Net income represents an increase in assets and owners' equity, while a net loss represents a decrease in assets and owners' equity.

A classified income statement contains the following sections:

Sales or Operating Revenues:	Net sales revenues (sales less returns) or service revenues are reported in this secttion (Key 30).
minus	
Cost of Goods Sold:	The amount the company paid for the inventory it sold. A service organization will not have this expense.
equals	
Gross Profit on Sales:	The difference between net sales revenues and the cost of goods sold. From this profit margin, the company must cover all other costs if it expects to have net income. A service organization will not report a "gross profit on sales."
minus	
Operating Expenses:	Selling and general and administrative expenses (Key 34). Service organizations will not divide their expenses between se-selling and general and administrative categories.
plus	
Other Revenues (Gains):	Increases in asset value from transactions not directly related to operations. For instance, interest earned on investments arises from a decision related to managing idle cash. That decision is not related to trying to earn a profit through sales or by providing services.
minus	
Other Expenses (Losses):	Decreases in asset value occur from transactions not directly related to operations. For instance, interest expense arises from the decision to finance operations by inc-icreasing debt. That decision is not related to trying to earn a profit through sales or by providing services.
equals	

Pretax Income from Continuing Operations:	The sum of all the revenues and expenses and expenses related to the portion of the business that is continuing.
minus	
Income Tax Expense:	A function of pretax income from continuing operations and the appropriate tax rates (see Key 37).
equals	
Income from Continuing Operations:	After-tax income of the portion of the business that is continuing.
plus or minus	
Discontinued Operations:	Either an after-tax gain or loss on a segment of the business that management in tends to sell (see Key 35).
equals	
Income Before Extraordinary Items:	A subtotal.
plus or minus	
Extraordinary Items:	After-tax gains or losses on unusual transactions (those not expected to recur) (see Key 36).
plus or minus	
Cumulative Effect of a Change in Accounting Principle:	A change in accounting principle occurs when management changes from one acceptable accounting to another. This is a catch-up adjustment. For example, suppose we change depreciation methods to a method that would have been recording more depreciation expense than we recorded under the old method. To catch the records up to where they would be if we had always used the new method we must take the additional depreciation in one lump. The amount of additional depreciation is the cumulative effect of the change in accounting principle.

When a company reports a change in accounting principle, it will also show pro forma income figures in a schedule attached to the income statement. These figures tell you what past net incomes would have been if the new principle had been used in those reporting years.

equals	
Net Income (loss):	The total of all reported revenues (gains) and expenses (losses).
Earnings Per Common Share:	Publicly traded companies are required to present several ratios that summarize the assumed income earned by each holder of a share of common share. Earnings per share ratios are the company's income divided by an average number of common shares assumed to be outstanding (see also Key 42).

An example of a classified income statement:

Consolidated Statements of Earnings

in thousands, except per share amounts	Year Ended November 30		
	1987	1986	1985
Net Sales	$598,149	$297,405	$267,321
Cost of goods sold	381,013	202,836	182,247
Gross profit	217,136	94,569	85,074
Selling, general and administrative expenses	152,076	69,383	65,521
Interest expense	15,426	1,860	2,458
Earnings from continuing operations before income taxes	49,634	23,326	17,095
Income taxes	26,263	11,698	8,579

Earnings from continuing operations	23,371	11,698	8,516
Loss from discontinued operations	—	—	(3,651)
Earnings before extraordinary item	23,371	11,628	4,865
Extraordinary item—termination of defined benefit pension plans, less applicable income taxes of $1,599	—	—	1,877
Net earnings	$ 23,371	$11,628	$ 6,742

Earnings per common share			
Primary			
Earnings from continuing operations	$ 1.15	$ .72	$ .53
Loss from discontinued operations	—	—	(.23)
Extraordinary item	—	—	.12
	$ 1.15	$ .72	$ .42
Fully diluted	$ 1.12	—	—

Average number of common shares outstanding			
Primary	20,293	16,225	16,201
Fully diluted	22,615	—	—

Red Flags. Not all income statements will include every section presented above. For instance, in a year in which a company does not have discontinued operations or a change in accounting principle, those sections will drop out of the income statement. Care should be taken when comparing income statements over time. Income from continuing operations is comparable to a later year's net income taken from an income statement that does not have discontinued operations, extraordinary items, or a change in accounting principle.

30

SALES AND OTHER REVENUES

Revenues (the money the company receives for its merchandise or services) are generally recorded at the time of sale or completion of the service. However, two conditions must be met before revenue can be recorded. First, the earnings process must be substantially complete, and (2) collectibility of the revenue can be estimated. The earnings process is not substantially complete if:

1. The seller and buyer have not agreed on the price of the merchandise or service
2. The buyer does not have to pay the seller until he resells the merchandise
3. The buyer does not have to pay the seller if the merchandise is stolen or physically destroyed
4. The buyer and seller are related parties (for example, parent and subsidiary)
5. The seller must still provide significant services to the buyer or aid in reselling the product

If substantial performance has occurred and the collectibility of the revenue can be estimated, the sale of the product or service can be recorded. (Key 31/BAD DEBTS discusses estimating the collectibility of credit sales and accounting for bad debts.) If a company cannot estimate the collectibility of a sale, it will record the revenue only as the customer makes payments. This has the effect of recording the sale on the basis of when the cash is received rather than when it is earned (the accrual basis—see Key 38). Accountants use either the installment method or the cost-recovery method to record revenue as the customer makes payments.

The installment method records part of each payment as revenue. Suppose we sold merchandise that cost us $4000 for $10,000. The gross profit on the sale is $6000 ($10,000 − $4,000) or 60% of the sales price ($6000 / $10,000). As the customer makes payments, $60 of each $100 collected will be reported as revenue. The revenue that has not yet been collected will be recorded as "Deferred Gross Profit" in the liability section of the balance sheet.

The cost-recovery method does not record revenue until the customer has paid the seller for his cost of the merchandise sold. Using the example given above, we would have to receive $4000 from the customer before any revenue would be recorded. After we recover the cost of the merchandise ($4000), each dollar received is recorded as revenue.

If a company provides services on a long-term contract, revenue may be recorded over the life of the contract. The construction industry records revenue on major long-term contracts as the work is performed rather than at the point of sale. If dependable estimates of selling price, construction costs, and stage of completion exist, the construction company will record revenue as the work is performed. Accountants call this the percentage-of-completion method.

For instance, suppose we are involved in a three-year construction project. The first year we estimate that we are one third complete. The second year we are two thirds complete.

Then we finish the project on schedule in the third year. We will record one third of the estimated gross profit (sales price less the total estimated construction cost) as revenue in the first year, another one third of the estimated gross profit in the second year (2/3 – 1/3 reported the first year), and the final one third as revenue in the third year.

While the percentage-of-completion method departs from the concept of recording revenue at the point of sale, it is consistent with the accrual concept of measuring activities in the period in which they occur. If a company does not have dependable estimates of the sales price, construction costs, or stage of completion, it will not recognize revenue until the project is complete (year 3 in our example).

A note to the financial statements showing the revenue components for a business segment is shown below.

Supplemental gaming segment operating data for the three years ended December 31, 1987 are as follows:

(In thousands)	1987	1986	1985
Revenue			
Rooms	$ 120,948	104,348	90,785
Food and Beverage	109,933	92,822	87,728
Casino	265,313	219,138	204,649
Promotional allowances	(34,921)	(27,891)	(26,637)
Other products and services	27,346	19,534	10,127
Total	488,619	407,951	366,652

31

BAD DEBTS

When a company accounts for bad debts, both the income statement and the balance sheet are affected. The estimate of bad debts is shown in the income statement. The estimate of uncollectible accounts is shown as a subtraction from total accounts receivable in the current assets section of the balance sheet (see Keys 13 and 14).

The key to understanding the accounting treatment of bad debts is to realize that the amounts involved are estimates of amounts that may be uncollectible. There are two goals in accounting for bad debts. One is to match the cost of bad debts to the sales revenue produced in the period. This means that, of necessity, some estimation must take place. At the end of the year, some credit sales will have resulted in accounts receivable that have already proven to be uncollectible. Other uncollected sales will not yet be known to be bad debts. An estimate of the uncollectible amount must be made if the company is to charge this year's profits with the bad-debts expense that result from this year's sales. If the company waits until each account proves to be uncollectible (or collectible), the costs of bad debts in one year may not be recognized until the next year. Bad-debts expense must be matched to the year benefited by the original sale. (The accounting concept of matching is explained in Key 5.)

The second goal in accounting for bad debts is to place a correct valuation on the amount of accounts receivable shown in the current assets section of the balance sheet. These accounts are all open; the company has not yet decided that any of them is definitely a bad debt. (When an account is judged to be uncollectible, it is removed from the accounts receivable.) As a result, the allowance for bad debts shown as a deduction from accounts receivable in the balance sheet is wholly an estimate. A note describing a reserve for bad debts is shown below.

Reserve for credit losses
The reserve for credit losses is established to absorb future losses from the credit portfolio based on management's judgment. Factors considered in determining the level of the reserve include industry concentrations, specific known risks, adequacy of collateral, past experience, the status and amount of nonaccrual, past due and restructured loans, off-balance sheet credit risks, and current as well as anticipated economic and political conditions that may affect certain borrowers. Credit losses are charged against the reserve; recoveries are added to the reserve.

Red Flags. There is some conflict between the two goals in accounting for bad debts—maximizing the accuracy of the income statement versus maximizing the accuracy of the balance sheet. Estimates of bad debts will occasionally be high or low, particularly on interim (quarterly) statements, but rarely on annual reports. To prevent misstatement, a company that does not relate the amount of bad debts expensed to sales activity will be required periodically to examine the outstanding accounts receivable in detail and justify the estimates that appear in the financial statements.

32

COST OF GOODS SOLD
AND INVENTORIES

Inventories were discussed in Key 15 as a component of the current assets section of the balance sheet. This key will help you understand the relationship between cost of goods sold in the income statement and the balance in inventory on hand in the balance sheet.

The total inventory available for sale each year is the total of the beginning inventory and the inventory purchased during the year. At year end, typically, part of the total inventory available for sale during the year is still on hand and part of it has been sold. The total cost of inventory available for sale is thus split between ending inventory in the balance sheet and the cost of goods sold in the income statement.

At first glance this may seem to be no problem. Indeed, if all units were purchased at the same price all year, there would be no problem. The problem is that most companies purchase units at many different prices, and, depending on the method used to flow costs through inventory, ending inventory and cost of goods sold can be any one of several different figures—all of which are acceptable for financial reporting!

The key to understanding inventory and cost of goods sold

is to realize that when units are identical, accountants are free to flow costs through the accounting records in ways that do not mimic the way the actual goods are handled.

To illustrate, assume that a company has no beginning inventory and purchases three *identical* units during the first quarter of the year: one in January, one in February, and one in March. The units are purchased for $4, $6, and $8 each. Now assume that one unit is sold for $10. What would the gross profit be?

If the company charges the $4 cost of the first unit purchased to cost of goods sold, gross profit would be $6 and ending inventory could be $14 ($6 + $8) for the two units still on hand. If the company charges the $6 cost of the second unit purchased to cost of goods sold, gross profit will be $4 and ending inventory will be $12 ($4 + $8). Finally, if the last unit purchased is expensed first, gross profit and ending inventory will be $2 and $10, respectively. These three alternatives are shown below.

	Alt. 1	Alt. 2	Alt. 3
In the income statement:			
Selling price	10	10	10
Cost of goods sold	4	6	8
	—	—	—
Gross Profit	6	4	2
In the balance sheet:			
Ending inventory	14	12	10
	(6 + 8)	(4 + 8)	(4 + 6)

The first possibility above would result if a company uses a FIFO (first-in, first-out) inventory flow. With FIFO, accountants flow costs the way merchants typically flow goods: the oldest units are sold first. The most recently purchased units are in ending inventory.

The third possibility results when a company uses the LIFO (last-in, first-out) method of inventory flow. Using LIFO, the cost of the most recent purchases are charged to cost of goods sold and the old costs remain in inventory, regardless of how the company flows the physical units.

The key to understanding the accounting logic behind LIFO inventory is to think about the result of the sale. How much better off is the company after selling one unit for $10? Is it $6 better off? Or $4? Or $2? To answer this question, we must think carefully. If the company is to remain in business, management must replace any units sold. How much will the next unit cost? The last purchase was for $8 per unit. Prices are rising ($4 to $6 to $8 per unit). The next, reasonably, will be for $8 per unit or more. If the company must replace the unit sold, the company is only $2 better off ($10 − $8 = $2), having sold one unit for $10. The logic that supports LIFO, flowing costs in a LIFO pattern regardless of the flow pattern of physical units, would increase the accuracy of the income statement.

The last possibility is a compromise between flowing costs as merchants flow inventory and maximizing the accuracy of the income statement. This method, called the Weighted Average Method, charges both ending inventory and cost of goods sold with the weighted average cost of all units available for sale. The weighted average cost per unit is $4 + $6 + $8 equals $18 divided by three units equals $6 per unit, as above.

Red Flags. The financial statement reader must realize that the use of different inventory methods results in financial statements that are not comparable. The inventories, cost of goods sold, and profit measures (gross profit and net income) of a company that uses LIFO cannot be compared to the same measures from a company that uses any other inventory method.

Many companies that use LIFO report lower earnings than companies using FIFO or weighted average. The LIFO company may, however, pay less tax (on the lower earnings) and, as a result, have much better cash flows than companies using other inventory methods. It is much better, all else being equal, to report lower earnings and pay less tax. LIFO gives a firm lower earnings and a tax advantage during inflationary periods when prices are rising.

33

MANUFACTURING COSTS

Manufacturing costs are considered assets and are part of the cost of manufactured units in inventory until the units are sold. When an assembly-line worker or factory foreman is paid, the wages are charged, not to a wage expense account, but directly, or through overhead, to an inventory of unfinished work in process (an asset). When prepaid insurance on the factory expires month by month, it is charged, not to insurance expense, but through overhead to an inventory of unfinished work in process (an asset).

There are three categories of manufacturing costs—labor, materials, and overhead—and they are all charged to the asset called work-in-process inventory. When financial statements are prepared, work-in-process inventory is shown in the current assets section of the balance sheet or is disclosed in the notes to the financial statements.

Manufacturing costs differ from nonmanufacturing costs in the timing of their charge against earnings. Nonmanufacturing costs, such as selling or administrative costs, are called *period costs* because they generally become expenses over a period of time. When a sales salary is paid, for example, it is immediately charged to sales salaries expense because the benefit of the salary was consumed in the period during which the salesperson made sales calls. When a year's insurance is paid on the corporate office building, however, the insurance cost is expensed month by month, as time passes, and the insurance (with its benefit as an asset) expires.

When units are completed, all the manufacturing costs charged to work-in-process inventory are transferred to finished-goods inventory, another asset account. Only when the finished goods are finally sold are the manufacturing costs transferred to an expense account, cost of goods sold. Because manufacturing costs are not expensed until the product is sold, manufacturing costs are called *product costs*.

The flow of manufacturing costs is illustrated below:

Raw materials used⎤
Direct Labor   ⎬ work-in-process → finished-goods → cost of goods
Factory overhead ⎦ inventory   inventory   sold(expense)

Factory overhead is the conglomeration of all the indirect costs of production, that is, all manufacturing costs except raw materials and labor used directly in the product. Factory overhead includes the costs of supervisory personnel, maintenance, factory and equipment depreciation, general supplies, energy, insurance, and any other manufacturing cost associated only indirectly with individual units produced.

Red Flags. The accounting method that charges all manufacturing costs to units produced is called *full* or *absorption costing*. Because absorption costing charges fixed capacity costs (such as supervision and factory depreciation) to individual units produced, net income is biased optimistically (high) when inventories are increasing, and pessimistically (low) when inventories are decreasing. The full explanation of why this happens is very complex, but the net effect is that in times of growth, when inventories are increasing, actual profits may not be quite as great as reported, and in times of recession, when inventories are shrinking, profits may not be as low as financial statements indicate.

34

OPERATING EXPENSES

In a financial statement, expenses (the costs of producing sales of products or services) are matched against the revenues they produce (see the discussion of matching in Key 5). Costs directly associated with producing a certain revenue are expensed in the same period that the revenue is recorded. The costs of long-lived assets, on the other hand, are expensed over the assets' expected lives (see Key 17/DEPRECIATION). Other costs that benefit only the current period are expensed as they arise.

In a business that sells merchandise, the major operating expense is the cost of merchandise sold (see Key 32/COST OF GOODS SOLD). This cost is recorded on the income statement below net sales. The difference between net sales and cost of goods sold is gross profit on sales, the profit margin that must cover all other costs if the company expects to have net income.

Other operating expenses are reported on the income statement after gross profit on sales (see Key 29/INCOME STATEMENT COMPONENTS). These operating expenses may be divided into selling and administrative expenses. *Selling expenses* are the costs associated with producing sales, and *administrative expenses* are the costs associated with managing the company.

The expenses listed are only representative of the types of costs that will be classified as selling or administrative expenses. In fact, few companies disclose the breakdown of their operating expenses. When a company does provide breakdowns, the actual costs and breakdowns may vary depending on the nature of the business. For instance, a service-oriented business may not break out its expenses into selling and administrative categories.

A schedule of operating expenses extracted from an income statement is shown below.

Salaries	$ 508	$ 480	$393
Employee benefits	78	99	117
Net occupancy expense	167	123	110
Equipment expense	93	91	68
Net expense of real estate acquired	94	12	6
Amortization of goodwill and other intangibles	43	27	16
Forms and supplies	34	32	29
Shares, capital and franchise taxes	22	18	14
Other expense	364	263	213
Total operating expense	$1,403	$1,145	$966

35

DISCONTINUED
OPERATIONS

The decision to discontinue a business operation creates a contingency, which we defined in Key 7 as a situation in which the company stands to gain or lose as the result of a past transaction or event. Only the amount of gain or loss is "contingent"—that is, dependent on another transaction or event. Whenever management decides to sell a segment of the business (the event giving rise to future gain or loss), a contingency is created. At that point, management may not know whether the sale will result in a gain or loss. Even if management has a buyer, the exact gain or loss may not be known until the disposal date.

Disclosure of discontinued operations follows the guidelines for disclosure of "likely" contingencies. If management expects a loss on disposal, that loss will be reported on the income statement in the period in which management makes the decision to sell. But if management expects a gain on the disposal, the gain will not be reported until the fiscal year in which the actual disposal occurs. Remember, conservatism governs the reporting of contingencies. Conservatism favors recording losses that are likely to occur before they occur, but recording gains when they actually occur.

Gains or losses on discontinued operations are reported in a special section of the income statement. That section follows income from continuing operations and precedes extraordinary items (see Key 29/INCOME STATEMENT COMPONENTS). Discontinued operations will be reported net of (including) their tax effects. Gains generally give rise to additional taxes, while losses generally result in tax savings. It is necessary to include all tax consequences in reporting discontinued operations because of the structure of the income statement. Income tax expense has been computed on income from continuing operations. To include in this calculation the one-time tax gain or loss from a sale would distort the income from continuing operations.

In the year in which management decides to sell the segment, two categories of discontinued operations may appear: first, gain or loss from operating the discontinued segment; second, gain or loss on disposal of the segment. The first figure is the segment's net income or loss from the beginning of the fiscal year to the date that management adopts the plan of disposal. The second figure is the contingency—the anticipated gain or loss, which includes the cost of winding down operations as well as actual disposal of the segment's assets.

Most dispositions will be reported on two income statements. Because disposal of a large business segment is a lengthy process, it is seldom accomplished within one fiscal period. Let's look at a simple example of a disposal.

Whatsit, Inc. decides to sell the Widget division to Wangsung, Ltd. The decision to sell is made at the October 1, 1988 board meeting. From January 1 to October 1, 1988 Widget experienced an after-tax loss of $1 million. Whatsit estimates that operations from October 1, 1988 until September 1, 1989 (the date Wangsung will take over operations) and the actual sale will generate a $5 million after-tax loss.

Whatsit's income statement for the year ended December 31, 1988 will show the following:

Discontinued Operations:

Loss from Operating Widget Division	$2,000,000
Estimated Loss on Disposal of Widget	5,000,000
	$7,000,000

Remember, the estimated loss on disposal is a contingency. Because Whatsit is estimating a loss, they will record it in the fiscal year in which the disposal decision was made. If Whatsit had estimated a gain on disposal, only the "Loss from Operating Widget Division" would be reported on the 1988 income statement. The gain would be recorded in 1989, when operations are actually turned over to Wangsung.

Because Whatsit must use estimates to recognize the "Loss on Disposal of Widget Division," any difference between the estimated loss and the actual loss will be reported in 1989. Suppose Whatsit experiences an actual after-tax loss on disposal of $5.7 million. The discontinued operations section of Whatsit's 1989 income statement would appear as follows:

Discontinued Operations:

Loss on Disposal of Widget Division	$700,000

Taken together, then, the 1988 and 1989 income statements report the full loss on disposal ($5.7 million).

Notice that Whatsit did not report any gain or loss from operating the Widget division during 1989. Any such gains or losses experienced after the decision to sell has been made are part of the gain or loss on disposal of the segment.

Now suppose that instead of the $5 million loss on disposal they estimated in 1988, Whatsit's actual loss was $4.8 million. The discontinued-operations section of Whatsit's 1989 income statement would appear as follows:

Discontinued Operations
Gain on Disposal of Widget Division $200,000

Together, the 1988 and 1989 income statements report the full loss on disposal of $4.8 million ($5 million estimated loss in 1988 minus the $200,000 gain reported in 1989).

Red Flags. Segregating gains or losses on discontinued operations on the income statement alerts the reader of the financial statements to the fact that a significant portion of the business will no longer be contributing to the company's earnings. In this situation, income from continuing operations (rather than net income) becomes the important figure when trying to forecast the future earning ability of the company.

Not all sales of business assets, segments, or divisions will be reported as discontinued operations. Only those operations that represent a completely separate line of product (service) or class of customer (client) are considered segments when reporting discontinued operations. For example, a U.S.-based gold mining operation that sells its mine in South Africa has not disposed of a segment or of a complete product line. Thus, no special report will be made. Gains or losses on disposal of business assets, segments, or divisions that do not represent a completely separate product line or class of customer will be reported as part of income from continuing operations.

36

EXTRAORDINARY ITEMS

Before a company can classify a gain or loss as an extraordinary item, two criteria must be met: the gain or loss will come from a transaction or event that is (1) unusual, and (2) nonrecurring. An *unusual transaction* or event is one that is unrelated to the typical activities of the business. A *nonrecurring transaction* or event is one that management does not expect to occur again.

The key to understanding extraordinary items is that both criteria must be met before a company can classify a gain or loss as extraordinary. The classification is company-specific. Natural disasters meet the definition of unusual (unrelated to the typical activities of the business). But, for an orange grower in North Florida a freeze would not be considered nonrecurring and could not be considered extraordinary. On the other hand, an earthquake in New York City would give rise to an extraordinary loss. The criteria of "unusual" and "nonrecurring" must be looked at from the perspective of the reporting company. Is the transaction or event unusual given the nature of that company's business and geographical location?

Presentation of Extraordinary Items. Extraordinary gains or losses are reported in their own section on the income statement, between discontinued operations and the cumulative effect of a change in accounting principle (see Key 29/ INCOME STATEMENT COMPONENTS). A net extraordinary gain (gain less additional income taxes) will increase income, while a net extraordinary loss (loss reduced by income tax savings) will decrease income. Accountants report extraordinary items net of their tax consequences. If a gain (or loss) is extraordinary, then so are the tax liabilities (or benefits) that it generates.

Segregating extraordinary gains or losses on the income statement is important. By classifying a gain or loss as extraordinary, management is saying "this is an unusual gain or loss and we do not expect it to recur." Comparability between fiscal years is gained by segregating extraordinary items. Because extraordinary items are not expected to recur, "Income Before Extraordinary Items" is a comparable figure to "Net Income" in years when there are no extraordinary gains or losses. Companies required to report earnings per share (see Key 42) will report these figures both "Before" and "After" "Extraordinary Items," so that there are easy comparisons for years that did not have extraordinary gains or losses.

A note relating to the presentation of an extraordinary item is shown below.

	1987	1986	1985
Income (loss) before extraordinary items and cumulative effect of change in accounting principle	232	699	(599)
Extraordinary items	—	(473)	18
Cumulative effect of change in accounting principle for reversion of surplus pension funds	—	270	—
Net income (loss)	$ 232	$ 496	$ (581)

As a result of the premium paid and expenses incurred in connection with the purchase of securities pursuant to the Debt Tender Offer (see Note 4), 1986 net income included an extraordinary charge of $473 million (after applicable taxes of $109 million), or $4.56 per share.

During 1985, the Corporation purchased $342 million of its outstanding long-term debt, resulting in an extraordinary net gain of $18 million (after applicable taxes of $15 million), or $0.08 per share.

Red Flags. Exceptions to evaluating gains and losses by the extraordinary criteria exist. Accounting principles require that certain types of gains and losses *not* be treated as extraordinary items, while other gains and losses *must* be treated as extraordinary items. Gains or losses that are not to be treated as extraordinary items include: (1) losses from the write-down or write-off of receivables, inventories, equipment, or intangible assets; (2) gains or losses related to foreign currency exchanges; (3) gains or losses from the sale of a business segment (see Key 35/DISCONTINUED OPERATIONS), (4) gains or losses from the sale or abandonment of property, plant, or equipment that has been used in the business; and (5) losses resulting from strikes by employees. These types of gains or losses may not receive extraordinary item treatment regardless of the company's line of business or geographical location. On the other hand, gains or losses on settlement of debt before its due date (the difference between the recorded value of the debt and the amount paid to settle the debt) must be reported as extraordinary items-again, without regard to the company's type of business or geographical location.

37

TAXES AND TAX DEFERRALS

The key to understanding tax deferrals is to realize that income tax regulations do not always require a company to use the same accounting method on the tax return that it has used on the income statement. Tax expense is related to the revenues and expenses listed on the income statement. In other words, taxes are recorded on the income statement in the same year that the revenues and expenses giving rise to the taxes are reported. This is the matching concept (see Key 5). However, the taxes currently due are related to the figures on the tax return. Accountants call the difference in these two amounts "deferred taxes."

Suppose a company decides to use a different method of depreciation on the income statement than it uses on the tax return. In such cases, depreciation expense on the income statement and on the tax return will be different at various times in the equipment's useful life. Consider this example:

Annual Depreciation

	Year 1	Year 2	Year 3	Year 4	Total
On Income Statement	$10,000	$10,000	$10,000	$10,000	$40,000
On Tax Return	$13,332	$17,780	$ 5,924	$ 2,964	$40,000
Difference*	($ 3,332)	($ 7,780)	$ 4,076	$ 7,036	$ -0-
Difference in Tax (30% rate)	($ 1,000)	($ 2,334)	$ 1,223	$ 2,111	$ -0-

* A negative difference (in parentheses) means that more depreciation will be recorded on the tax return, decreasing the amount of taxes currently due.

In years 1 and 2, this company will record more depreciation on the tax return than on the income statement ($3332 and $7780 more, respectively). This will cause it to pay less in tax than it is showing as tax expense on its income statement ($1000 and $2334 less, respectively). In effect, by claiming more depreciation on the tax return, the company is postponing taxes in years 1 and 2.

In years 3 and 4, the company will show more depreciation on the income statement than on the tax return ($5924 and $2964 more, respectively). This will cause it to pay more taxes than are showing in tax expense for years 3 and 4 ($1223 and $2111 more, respectively). This is the payment of the postponed taxes from years 1 and 2.

You will notice that there is no difference between the income statement and the tax return in total depreciation taken over the four years. Over that same period tax expense will also equal the amount of taxes due. The difference is simply in the timing of the payments and of the reporting.

In the example above, a liability is created in years 1 and 2 for future taxes. This liability is paid in years 3 and 4. The balance sheet prepared at the end of year 1 will show the deferred tax liability as noncurrent (it will not come due in the next year). The balance sheet prepared at the end of year 2 will show $1223 of the deferred tax liability as current (the amount that will come due in the next year) and $2111 as a noncurrent (the amount that does not come due until year 4).

Recording revenues and expenses on the income statement and tax return in different periods can also produce a deferred tax asset. Suppose that our fiscal year ends on December 31 and that in December 1988 we collect January 1989 rents. Income tax regulations require that we pay tax on the rents in 1988, the year in which they are collected. Under the accrual concept (see Key 5), the rents are not earned until January 1989 even though they must be reported as revenue on the 1988 tax return. Since the rents are unearned, they will be reported as a current liability on the December 31, 1988 balance sheet. The 1988 tax payment will be more than the expense showing on the income statement. We have paid taxes on revenue we have received but have not yet earned (we still owe the tenants occupancy for January or their money back). This prepayment will be treated as a deferred tax asset.

If the company experiences a change in tax rates from one year to the next, it must revise the recorded amount of the deferred tax liability or deferred tax asset. This adjustment will be made through tax expense. Suppose the income statement shows $10,000 more in revenue than the tax return. At a 30% rate this will create a $3000 deferred tax liability. If the tax rate increases to 40%, this will require the deferred tax liability to be increased by $1000 ($10,000 × 40% – $3,000). This adjustment will be made by increasing income tax expense by $1000 when the tax rate changes. Tax rates can change either by legislation or because the company moves into a higher (or lower) tax bracket through changes in earnings.

A company should use timing differences to its advantage. Where income tax regulations allow, it can use methods on the tax return that will minimize the amount of taxes currently due, thus creating a deferred tax liability. The advantage of postponing as long as legally possible the payment of tax is that the company then can use those funds to earn additional profits.

A note giving the components of income and taxes and explaining the deferred taxes for the year is shown below.

7. Taxes on income

	Year ended May 31		
	1987	1986	1985
	(In millions)		
Earnings before taxes on income consists of:			
Domestic	$329.1	$349.6	$318.8
Foreign	23.4	27.5	21.4
	$352.5	$377.1	$340.2
Taxes on income consists of:			
Current:			
Federal	$ 76.9	$127.4	$113.8
Investment tax credit	2.7	(8.2)	(9.0)
	79.6	119.2	104.8
State	11.2	19.4	16.8
Foreign	7.4	6.9	1.5
	98.2	145.5	123.1
Deferred:			
Federal	63.1	16.8	22.3
State	8.1	2.7	2.4
Foreign	1.2	4.0	.6
	72.4	23.5	25.3
	$170.6	$169.0	$148.4

38

ACCRUAL ACCOUNTING
VERSUS CASH FLOW

The *accrual principle* attempts to translate into dollars of profit or loss the actual activities of the fiscal period. The accrual principle is a combination of two ideas, revenue recognition and matching.

The *revenue recognition principle* provides that revenue (sales price) be recorded when the necessary activities to sell a good or provide a service have been completed. Revenue is recorded at the time of sale regardless of whether cash is collected or a receivable from the customer is created at that time.

The *matching principle* tells the accountant when to record a production cost as an expense. Costs directly associated with producing a certain revenue will be expensed in the same period that the revenue is recorded. But the cost of long-lived assets will be expensed over their expected lives, and other costs that benefit only the current period are expensed as they arise.

Under the matching principle an expense can be recorded before, after, or at the time a cost is actually paid. From the accountant's point of view it is the earnings activity that gives rise to the conversion of cost to expense—it does not matter whether that cost has been paid or a liability created.

Cash basis reporting is concerned only with the business's checkbook. Cash inflows are treated as revenues of the period; cash outflows are treated as the period's expenses. These cash flows do not capture the earnings activities of the period. For instance, we may have sold merchandise to a customer at the end of the year. Thus the customer will not pay us until next year. On the cash basis, the sale will not be recorded until the collection is made in the new year even though the effort to generate the sale was made in the old year. Likewise, if the salesman will not be paid for that day's work until the next period, his salary is not yet expensed on the cash basis.

Red Flags. Accrual accounting provides a measure of a period's earnings activities. Comparing accrual income measures over time can give us a feel for what the company can do in the future. But it does not provide us with a measure of the company's liquidity—its ability to pay its debts as they come due.

Cash-flow accounting will not isolate the earnings activities of a period. However, it does provide us with a liquidity measure.

If we combine accrual-income measures with cash-flow measures, we have a base from which to estimate future operations, measure liquidity, and determine the timing between producing sales and collecting on sales. This combination takes place when we use both the income statement (see Key 29) as well as the statement of cash flows (see Key 39) in analyzing a company's financial health.

39

STATEMENT OF CASH FLOWS

The statement of cash flows is like a bridge. Balance sheets tell us what a company's assets, liabilities, and owners' equity are at a point in time. But what about the changes that have occurred in the business between two balance sheet dates (from the end of one fiscal year to the end of another)? The statement of cash flows is this bridge. It describes all of the changes that have occurred in the balance sheet during the fiscal year in terms of their effect on cash. What changes in the assets, liabilities, and owners' equity provided cash? What changes in assets, liabilities, and owners' equity used cash? These are the questions that are answered by a statement of cash flows.

Here is one format that is used in presenting the statement of cash flows.

XYZ, Ltd.
Statement of Cash Flows
For the Year Ended December 31, 1988

Cash Flows From Operating Activities:		
Received from customers	$2,418,500	
Paid suppliers and employees	(1,255,000)	
Dividends and interest received	150,000	
Interest paid	(260,500)	
Taxes paid	(320,000)	
Net cash provided by operating activities		$733,000
Cash Flows From Investing Activities:		
Received—sale of plant	3,000,000	
Received—sale of equipment	550,000	
Paid—new equipment purchases	(1,015,000)	
Paid—new plant	(4,950,000)	
Net cash used in investing activities		(2,415,000)
Cash Flows From Financing Activities:		
Received—sale of bonds	2,000,000	
Paid—dividends to shareholders	(90,000)	
Net cash provided by investing activities		1,910,000
Net Increase in Cash		228,000
Cash at the Beginning of the Year		50,000
Cash at the End of the Year		$ 278,000

"Net cash provided (used) by operating activities" is cash-basis net income (see Key 38). It includes all collections during the year from sales of merchandise or from providing services along with all dividends and interest received from investments, reduced by the payment of operating costs, including interest and taxes. A schedule reconciling accrual-based net income for the year to the cash collected from

111

operating activities must accompany the statement of cash flows.

"Net cash provided (used) by investing activities" relates to changes in the company's assets. Decreases in investments, property, plant and equipment, intangibles, or other assets indicate that sales have taken place, providing the company with cash. Increases in these same assets indicate that the company has purchased additional assets—a major use of cash.

"Net cash provided (used) by financing activities" relates to changes in the company's liabilities or owners' equity. Increasing debt or selling stock (ownership) will provide the company with cash. Decreasing liabilities (indicating payment of debt) and dividends to shareholders are major uses of cash.

Some transactions do not have a direct effect on cash. For example, a purchase of land on a long-term mortgage with no cash down payment does not affect the company's cash balance. However, for the statement of cash flows to be a complete bridge between two balance sheets (describing all the changes that have occurred in assets, liabilities, and owners' equity), this transaction must be reported. Major investing and financing activities that do not directly affect cash will be summarized in a schedule that accompanies the statement of cash flows.

40

CONSOLIDATED FINANCIAL STATEMENTS

The key to understanding consolidated financial statements is to realize that they are more or less the sum of the parts. They are the combined financial statements of a parent company and its subsidiaries. A parent/subsidiary relationship is created when a company acquires more than 50% of the common stock of another company. Because common stock is the voting stock of a corporation, acquiring more than 50% entitles the acquiring company (parent) to majority representation on the board of directors of the acquired company (subsidiary) and, thus, to control the affairs of that company.

Accounting principles require that the assets, liabilities, revenues, and expenses of majority-owned subsidiaries be included in the financial statements of their parents. In preparing the combined (consolidated) financial statements, accountants eliminate any transactions between the parent and its subsidiaries. If these transactions were not eliminated, the assets, liabilities, revenue, and expense of the combined company would be overstated.

For example, if the parent Z has lent $5 million to its Subsidiary X, it will have a $5 million "Receivable from

Subsidiary X" (an asset) recorded. Subsidiary X will have a $5 million "Payable to Parent Z" (a liability) recorded. But because parent and subsidiary are treated as one company in the consolidated financial statements, it makes no sense to report these items. A company cannot borrow from, or owe to, itself. When the consolidated balance sheet is prepared, the parent's $5 million receivable will be canceled against the subsidiary's $5 million payable. If this were not done, consolidated assets and liabilities would each be reported as $5 million more than they actually are.

In consolidating the financial statements of a parent and its subsidiaries that are not wholly owned (the parent does not own 100% of the voting stock), "minority interest" is created. "Minority interest" is the owners' equity held by the other shareholders of the subsidiary. If parent Z owns 60% of Subsidiary X, there is a 40% minority interest. Because accounting principles will allow all of the assets and liabilities of a subsidiary to be reported in the consolidated financial statements, the portion of those assets and liabilities that "belong" to the minority shareholders must be labeled "minority interest." "Minority interest" may be shown on the consolidated balance sheet either as a liability (the amount the parent "owes" the minority shareholders) or as a part of consolidated owners' equity.

Another account that frequently appears on the consolidated balance sheet is "Excess of Cost Over Net Assets Acquired." This is purchased goodwill (see Key 18), an intangible asset that will be amortized (expensed) over a period of time not to exceed 40 years (see Key 19/AMORTIZATION). Additional information on the activities of the subsidiaries will be included in the notes to the financial statements dealing with "segments." A business segment can be defined as a major product line, an industry, a class of customer, domestic operations, or foreign operations.

A consolidated balance sheet showing minority interest between stockholders' equity and noncurrent liabilities is shown below.

Consolidated Statement of Financial Position
December 31, 1987 and 1986

millions of dollars		1987	1986
Assets			
Current assets	Cash	$188	$116
	Marketable securities—at cost, which approximates market	1,328	325
	Accounts and notes receivable (less allowances of $82 on December 31, 1987, and $89 on December 31, 1986)	2,751	2,554
	Inventories	899	865
	Prepaid expenses and income taxes	393	340
		5,559	4,200
Investments and other assets	Investments and related advances	606	680
	Long-term receivables and other assets	533	657
		1,139	1,137
Properties	—at cost, less accumulated depreciation, depletion, and amortization of $16,789 on December 31, 1987, and $15,381 on December 31, 1986	18,129	18,169
		$24,827	$23,706

Liabilities and Shareholders' Equity

Current liabilities	Current installments of long-term obligations	$222	$236
	Short-term obligations	165	174
	Accounts payable	2,543	2,289
	Accrued liabilities	998	872

	Taxes payable (including income taxes)	970	1,019
		4,898	4,590
Long-term obligations	Debt	2,773	2,993
	Capitalized leases	308	327
		3,081	3,320
Deferred credits and other non-current liabilities	Income taxes	4,238	3,997
	Other	497	469
		4,735	4,466
Minority interest		6	6
Shareholders' equity	Common stock (authorized 800,000,000 shares; issued and outstanding as of December 31, 1987—257,634,285 shares; December 31, 1986—255,700,810 shares)	2,114	1,875
	Earnings retained and invested in business	10,044	9,610
	Foreign currency translation adjustment	(51)	(161)
	Total shareholders' equity	12,107	11,324
		$24,827	$23,706

41

QUARTERLY STATEMENTS

Both the New York Stock Exchange and the Securities and Exchange Commission (SEC) require that listed or registered companies provide their shareholders with quarterly financial statements. The content of the quarterly report filed with the SEC (the 10-Q) is discussed in Key 11. Quarterly financial statements are prepared for the first three quarters of a company's fiscal year. Fourth-quarter statements are unnecessary because annual financial statements will be issued at that time.

Quarterly financial statements look much the same as annual financial statements. However, there are some major differences. Accounting principles require that the same methods of recording revenue, expense, assets, and liabilities be used in the quarterly statements as will be used to prepare the annual statements, but in quarterly reports it is necessary to estimate most key figures. For instance, because taking a physical inventory count is time consuming and costly, it will be done only annually. In order to prepare the quarterly financial statements, ending inventory for the quarter will be estimated. The annual tax rate must also be estimated so that quarterly taxes can be recorded at the rate the company actually expects to pay.

Accounting principles also require that seasonality in the quarterly statements be pointed out. For instance, suppose that the second quarter's sales are normally greater than other quarters' sales. This should be pointed out in the second quarter's financial statements. This has the effect of reminding the reader that sales are not level throughout the year.

Finally, quarterly financial statements are unaudited. The CPA merely reviews the statements, saying nothing more than "I do not know of any material changes which must be made to make the statements conform to Generally Accepted Accounting Principles" (see Key 9 for a discussion of GAAP). But, the accountant has not made tests of the underlying accounting records to see if they support the figures in the financial statements—that would be an audit. (See Key 10 for a discussion of the difference between an audit and a review.)

42

EARNINGS PER SHARE

The key to understanding earnings per share (eps) is to realize that it is a simple, almost intuitive accounting measure carried (of necessity) to its most complicated, confusing extreme. Accounting Principles Board Opinion 15 requires that a publicly held company calculate and report its earnings per share. But Opinion 15 was so complicated and confusing as issued that an official explanation—over 100 pages long— was written to help accountants understand the original opinion. Still, earnings per share is important—it is often cited as the single most used financial ratio—and you can understand it if you ignore the complications and concentrate on the purpose of this ratio.

Earnings per share is simply the earnings of the company divided by the number of shares of stock outstanding. When you examine a company's earnings over a period of several years, a pattern of growth or contraction may become apparent. Reducing the company's total earnings to a measure of earnings per ownership share helps an investor determine how successful the company is in creating earnings for individual shareholders. If a company sells additional shares of stock, for instance, you would expect total earnings to increase as a result of the additional investment received from owners. The additional shareholder investment might be used to build a plant or expand operations in some other way.

An increase in total earnings achieved in this way can be misleading. Suppose a company with 100,000 shares of stock outstanding issued an additional 20,000 shares of stock and expanded production facilities with the cash received. Assume, as a result, that the company's earnings increased from $200,000 to $220,000 per year. If an investor looks only at total earnings, an increase of 10% may appear good. But if we look at the earnings per share for the two years, we see a decrease:

Before investment eps = $200,000/100,000 shares = $2.00 per share
After investment eps = $220,000/120,000 shares = $1.83 per share

As companies increase and decrease the number of shares outstanding—by issuing or retiring shares of stock, by combining with other companies, or by fulfilling obligations to convert bonds or to meet employee stock options—the eps figure relates the company's reported earnings to the number of shares of stock outstanding. The basic equation for earnings per share is:

$$\text{basic eps} = \frac{\text{earnings}}{\text{number of shares}}$$

But now for the complications: Suppose there are preferred stockholders as well as common stockholders. If that is the case, some of the company's earnings must be paid as dividends to preferred stockholders just as interest must be paid on debt. Dividend payments to preferred stockholders are a cost of capital (like interest) and must be subtracted from earnings to determine the earnings available to common stockholders. (Interest is already deducted as an operating expense in calculating earnings.) So, if we are interested in the earnings per share for common stockholders, we must modify the eps equation to read:

$$\text{eps} = \frac{\text{earnings available to common stockholders}}{\text{number of shares}}$$

Suppose further that the company issued or retired common stock during the year. A correct calculation now requires that a weighted average number of shares be used as the denominator. (This average weighs shares by the number of months they are outstanding during the year. This takes into account whether the shares were issued near the beginning or end of the year.)

$$\text{eps} = \frac{\text{earnings available to common stockholders}}{\text{weighted average number of shares}}$$

When a company has issued preferred stock or bonds that are convertible to shares of common stock, or when it has stock warrants or options outstanding that entitle the holders to purchase stock, the calculation of eps becomes even more complex. Some of these items are essentially shares of common stock in that it is obvious that at some point they will be exercised and increase the number of shares outstanding. By the same token, it may be obvious that other items will never be exercised and thus will not result in an increase in common stock outstanding. On some items, of course, even experts would disagree.

To calculate a useful measure of eps, the number of shares should be increased to reflect the increase that will result from those items that are essentially shares of common stock. (These items are called common stock equivalents.) The number of shares should not be increased to include those items that will never be exercised. Those that may be exercised (but are not common stock equivalents) could cause some confusion. When they are present, accountants calculate two measures of eps and publish both of them with the income statement in the annual report. The two measures of eps are called *primary* earnings per share (containing only a weighted average of common shares and common stock equivalents in the denominator) and *fully diluted* earnings per share (with all items that could reasonably be converted to common stock counted as common shares.

It must be noted that when accountants treat an item as if

it were converted into common stock—thus increasing the number of shares outstanding—an adjustment must frequently also be made to the numerator. For example, if an issue of convertible bonds is treated as if the bonds were converted into common stock, the accountant must also correct earnings by adding back the interest expense that would not have been subtracted if the bonds had actually been converted. Similar corrections must also be made for dividends holders of convertible preferred shares.

An example of the income statement presentation of earnings per share is shown below.

Earnings per common share			
Primary			
Earnings from continuing operations	$ 1.15	$ .72	$ .53
Loss from discontinued operations	—	—	(.23)
Extraordinary item	—	—	.12
	$ 1.15	$ .72	$ .42
Fully diluted	$ 1.12	—	—
Average number of common shares outstanding			
Primary	20,293	16,225	16,201
Fully diluted	22,615	—	—

Red Flags. Accountants must often use reference materials to guide them in making these calculations. For the layman, trying to follow eps calculations can be quite confusing. Fully diluted eps is the most complex calculation, being an attempt to reflect the effect of every event that would (if it happened) result in a reduction of eps.

Many analysts place special emphasis on the trend of a company's eps from quarter to quarter or year to year. While this trend may well be more useful than the absolute value of the eps in any one period, a financial statement reader would be well advised to treat this measure as any other ratio and apply the analysis approach discussed in Key 50.

4 divided by 3
4/3
4:3
4 to 3
1.33

The expressions above all show the ratio of four to three, but they are also the ratio of any other pair of numbers where the first is 1-1/3 times the second. The expressions above also are the ratio of 400 to 300, or 4 million to 3 million, or 12,000 to 9000 or 992 to 744, and so on. A ratio describes the relative size of two numbers or quantities but does not tell you the absolute size of the quantities being described. Each of the pairs listed, expressed as a fraction, reduces to 4/3, or, divided, equals 1.33.

A ratio also gives information about the two quantities used to generate the ratio. Assume the ratio of weight (in pounds) to height (in feet) for Bill Jones is 45:1. Can you make judgments about Bill based only on this ratio? Would Bill be a good pick for a basketball team? Using the ratio, we know that if Bill weighs 225 pounds, he is 5 feet tall (225/5 reduces to 45/1, or the ratio expressed as 45:1, above). At 6 feet tall, Bill would have to weigh 270 pounds ($6 \times 45 = 270$) to have a weight-to-height ratio of 45:1. So Bill is probably not a good pick for a basketball team. For a football lineman, however, Bill may be a great pick! You cannot tell for sure, because you do not know the absolute values for his weight or height, but you can begin to form judgments from the relative measure of weight to height. Bill is a better pick for a football lineman, for instance, than is Ted Jones, whose weight-to-height ratio is 35:2. At 6 feet tall, Ted would weigh only 105 pounds ($35 \times 6/2 = 105$).

The same basic idea holds true for using ratios to make assessments of financial statements. Assume a company has assets of $10 million and liabilities of $6 million. The ratio of assets to liabilities is 5:3 (10:6 reduces to 5:3). What judgments can you make from this ratio? Is the company solvent?

Yes, the company is solvent, for assets are greater than liabilities. (The ratio of assets to liabilities is greater than one.) But does the company have an ideal level of debt? Should the company have more debt? Or less debt? Without a standard of comparison, you cannot tell. Above, when you were told "basketball team" or "football lineman," you had a standard of reference to judge Bill, for you know the general build of these players. Or, when you were given Ted as a comparison to Bill, you could make judgments about Bill's relative desirability. The same is true of ratio analysis for companies. If you know the general ratio for assets to liabilities for the company's industry (a standard of reference) or for its major competitor (a comparison), you can make a judgment as to the desirability of an asset-to-liability ratio of 5:3.

A ratio for a company can be compared to each of the following: (1) the company's industry average or standard, (2) another company in the same industry, or (3) the same ratio for the company in prior years.

A comparison with ratios of prior years gives a different perspective than does a comparison with ratios for the company's industry or competitor. A comparison with prior years may disclose a pattern. Assume, for instance, that the ratio of assets to liabilities for a company has gone from 5:2 to 2:1 to 5:3 during the last three years. Debt has increased— from 40% to 50% to 60% of total assets. Depending on other factors, this may be a cause of great concern.

Finally, you should note that more than one ratio is needed to make an assessment of the financial statements in a company's annual report. Ratios are available that help in analyzing profitability, solvency, activity, and liquidity. These ratios are described and analyzed in the succeeding four sections. A company's solvency ratios may be ideal, but if ratios that help analyze profitability and activity are bad (profits are down and sales are stagnant), a financial analyst would be concerned. You can only learn to use ratios in financial statement analysis by diving in and doing a bit of hard work. That is the key to understanding ratio analysis!

44

PROFITABILITY RATIOS

Profitability ratios are usually "return on" ratios, measuring some aspect of management's operating efficiency. The numerator (the figure above the line) of a profitability ratio is usually some measure of net income or profit, and the denominator (the figure below the line) some aspect of the company that is management's responsibility. Profitability ratios relate profit to some particular aspect of management performance—return on assets, return on owners' investment (or equity), or return on sales. Profitability ratios that measure management's performance on these three areas follow. To measure management's success in employing assets profitably:

$$\text{return on assets} = \frac{\text{net income}}{\text{total assets}}$$

To measure management's success in maximizing the return on owners' investment:

$$\text{return on equity} = \frac{\text{net income}}{\text{owners' equity}}$$

To evaluate the profit generated on sales:

$$\text{return on sales} = \frac{\text{net income}}{\text{sales}}$$

Frequently the return-on-sales ratio is combined with the asset-turnover ratio so that the components of the return-on-assets profitability ratio can be studied. (Asset turnover can be defined simply as the number of times an asset is replaced during the period being analyzed.) The combination of these equations is called the DuPont method of financial analysis:

$$\text{return on sales} \times \text{asset turnover} = \text{return on assets}$$

$$\frac{\text{net income}}{\text{sales}} \times \frac{\text{sales}}{\text{assets}} = \frac{\text{net income}}{\text{assets}}$$

Depending on the firm and the industry, a company may stress either the return (or margin) on sales or the turnover and still generate the same return on assets. Imagine a giant new car dealership with high turnover and low prices, and a tiny dealership with low turnover and higher prices. Both might generate the same return on total assets.

	return on sales		asset turnover		return on assets
giant dealer:	.05	×	6	=	.30
tiny dealer:	.15	×	2	=	.30

Another class of profitability ratios relates the earnings reported by the company to the price of its stock or the dividend pattern established by management.

$$\text{price earnings (PE) ratio} = \frac{\text{common stock market price}}{\text{earnings per common share}}$$

$$\text{dividend-payout ratio} = \frac{\text{dividend per common share}}{\text{earnings per common share}}$$

Both of these ratios are important to analysts. The price-earnings ratio helps an analyst decide whether the stock is overpriced or underpriced in the market for the income the company is reporting. The PE ratio is considered so important that it is listed in the stock tables published daily in *The Wall Street Journal* and general newspapers with large financial sections. The dividend-payout ratio helps an analyst determine what management is doing with the earnings produced by operations: paying out a high proportion in dividends to yield greater current income to shareholders; using the earnings to finance company growth, and holding out the possibility of greater future profits; or using a balanced approach. Both of these ratios are important in establishing the price of the company's stock in the market.

45

ACTIVITY RATIOS

Activity ratios measure management's effectiveness in using assets. These ratios generally involve a measure of the relationship between some asset, such as accounts receivable, and some surrogate for management's ability to employ the investment in the asset effectively.

The key to understanding activity ratios is to note that the general form of these ratios is an asset divided into the best measure of that asset's activity. The general form is:

$$\text{Activity Ratio} = \frac{\text{Best Measure of Asset Activity}}{\text{Asset}}$$

For accounts receivable, the best measure of the asset activity is sales. The less money tied up in uncollected accounts for a given volume of sales, the more money management will have for other purposes. In a company with annual sales of $1 million and $500,000 in accounts receivable at the end of the year, for instance, management's performance would be improved if more sales' dollars could be collected and accounts receivable reduced to $100,000.

Activity ratios are usually referred to as *turnover ratios*. Accounts receivable of $100,000 is said to have turned over ten times in a company with annual sales of $1 million. For a company that does credit business, all sales go through accounts receivable, like water through a water wheel. For sales to pass through accounts receivable $100,000 at a time (the average balance), accounts receivable would "turn over" ten times. The activity ratio "accounts receivable turnover" is:

$$\text{AR turnover} = \frac{\text{Sale}}{\text{Average AR}}$$

In the example above, the ratio is calculated as $1 million divided by $100,000 equals 10 times. When the turnover of accounts receivable is known, the average collection period (average time funds are tied up in the asset) can be calculated. If accounts receivable turn over 10 times in a 360-day year (a banker's year), the average collection period is 360 divided by 10 equals 36 days.

$$\text{Average turnover period} = \frac{360}{\text{Asset turnover}}$$

This relationship can also be used to calculate the number of days funds are tied up in any other asset once the asset turnover is known. Other common activity or turnover ratios are listed below.

$$\text{inventory turnover} = \frac{\text{cost of goods sold}}{\text{average inventory}}$$

$$\text{fixed-assets turnover} = \frac{\text{sales}}{\text{average fixed assets}}$$

$$\text{total-asset turnover} = \frac{\text{sales}}{\text{average total assets}}$$

46

LIQUIDITY RATIOS

There are only two liquidity ratios in common usage. Both of these ratios are designed to evaluate the company's ability to pay its short-term obligations.

The first liquidity ratio is the *current ratio*, which is simply the relationship between current assets and current liabilities.

$$\text{current ratio} = \frac{\text{current assets}}{\text{current liabilities}}$$

Current assets are short-term assets that either are cash or will become cash in one year. Examples are receivables that will be collected in 90 days or inventory on hand that will be sold in the next quarter. Current liabilities are short-term debts that must be paid in one year or less. Any part of a long-term debt that comes due in the next 12 months is also a current liability. Thus, accounts payable and next year's installment on a 40 year mortgage are both considered current liabilities.

The second common liquidity ratio is called the *quick* or *acid test ratio*.

$$\text{quick ratio} = \frac{\text{current assets - inventory}}{\text{current liabilities}}$$

In the quick ratio, inventory is removed from current assets because inventory is usually not directly convertible to cash. Generally, inventory is sold to create an account receivable, and the receivable must then be collected before cash is available to pay short-term creditors.

The rule of thumb is 2:1 for the current ratio and 1:1 for the quick ratio. These rules of thumb are often cited but are, in fact, relatively useless. To have meaning, a ratio either must be compared to the ratios of other companies in the same industry, or must be viewed as part of a trend for a particular company. An analyst must ask questions: Is the company's liquidity (current ratio) increasing or decreasing? If so, are the changes appropriate for the economic climate in the company's industry? Sources of industry averages are cited in Key 50.

47

OVERALL (DEBT AND EQUITY) RATIOS

The overall (debt and equity) ratios are sometimes called solvency ratios. While liquidity ratios assist analysts in examining a company's ability to pay short-term debt, overall or solvency ratios indicate the relative size of the claims of long-term creditors, compared to the claims or property rights of owners.

The existence of too much long-term debt places restrictions on management and increases risk to stockholders. Long-term debt increases the fixed charges against income each period. The times interest earned (TIE) or the fixed charge coverage ratios, both of which are defined below, assist analysts in evaluating the burden on a company's finances of fixed interest and other periodic charges (lease payments, for example). These ratios are similar to the rules of thumb that limit a consumer's house payment, or house and car payments, to a certain percentage of the consumer's income. The proportion of a company's income that can safely be consumed by interest and other fixed charges, however, varies widely, depending on conditions within each company and within the industry in which the company operates.

Another effect of high levels of long-term debt is added risk to creditors. As long-term debt increases, creditors grow reluctant to continue to lend the company money. Eventually, funds will not be available or will be available only at very high interest rates.

The common ratios used to evaluate a company's solvency or overall debt and equity position are as follows:

$$\text{times interest earned (or interest coverage)} = \frac{\text{earnings before interest and taxes}}{\text{interest expense}}$$

$$\text{fixed charge coverage} = \frac{\text{earnings before interest and taxes}}{\text{interest expense} + \text{lease payments}}$$

$$\text{debt to total assets} = \frac{\text{debt}}{\text{total assets}}$$

$$\text{debt to total equity} = \frac{\text{debt}}{\text{total liabilities} + \text{stockholders' equity}}$$

$$\text{debt to stockholders' equity} = \frac{\text{debt}}{\text{stockholders' equity}}$$

Red Flags. As mentioned above, too much long-term debt can be bad. This fact may bias readers of annual reports against long-term debt. But companies do not borrow without the desires of stockholders in mind. Managers use long-term debt to increase returns to common stockholders through financial leverage, as explained in Key 48. Long-term debt is not of itself bad, any more than using a mortgage to purchase a home is bad. The danger in both instances is in the level of total indebtedness and the burden of the resulting fixed payments.

48

OPERATING AND FINANCIAL LEVERAGE

Leverage seems more properly a subject for a book on physics. There, it would be explained that when a lever is properly placed across a fulcrum, downward pressure on the handle results in a greatly magnified upward force on the other end. Ten pounds of downward pressure may be sufficient to lift a 100-pound weight. A child may lift a boulder with a lever, which gives the child a mechanical advantage.

There are two kinds of leverage managers can use to increase the profitability of a business to its owners: operating leverage and financial leverage. Both are very similar in principle to a child lifting a rock with a lever.

Operating Leverage. A company uses operating leverage to its advantage by balancing the mix of fixed and variable costs in its operations. Assume a company manufactures a product that it sells for $10. The labor and raw material costs for each unit of product (both are variable costs) total $8. Using a lot of labor, the company can manufacture the product with fixed costs (largely related to machinery) of only $20,000 per year. This is a fixed cost, remaining stable regardless of the number of units produced. With this balance of fixed costs and variable costs, each unit of product contributes $2 to covering the fixed costs and to building profits.

Selling price	$10
Labor and raw material	8
Contribution per unit	$ 2

Assume now that the company's managers decide to automate several previously manual operations. This increases the annual fixed machinery cost to $50,000, but the cost of labor and raw materials per unit is decreased to $6. Now each unit contributes $4 to covering fixed charges and to profit.

Selling price	$10
Labor and raw material	6
Contribution per unit	$ 4

Leverage increases the impact of a change in sales volume on the company's profits. Consider the contribution to profits of a 1,000-unit increase in sales

Manual Operation		Automated Operation	
Selling price	$10	Selling price	$10
Labor and raw material	8	Labor and raw material	6
Contribution per unit	$ 2	Contribution per unit	$ 4
Increased units	×1,000	Increased units	× 1,000
Contribution	$2,000	Contribution	$4,000

Changing the variable labor cost of operations to a fixed machinery cost has increased the contribution of a 1,000-unit sale from $2,000 to $4,000. The automation has "leveraged" the effect of a sales increase on company profit.

Red Flag. Operating leverage has a down side. For instance, assume that instead of a 1,000-unit increase in sales, the company had a 1,000-unit decrease in sales volume. The effect is still the same dollar amount, but now the $2,000 and $4,000 changes in contribution are decreases, not increases.

Thus, highly leveraged companies generally have greater fluctuations in profits than companies with low operating leverage. A low-leveraged, manual operation does not benefit as much from increases in sales, but neither does it suffer as much from declines. Profits, by and large, will remain fairly stable. An automated, highly leveraged company, in contrast, will benefit greatly from sales increases and will suffer greatly from sales decreases. The contribution lost or gained will be greater, and the pattern of profits less stable.

Another warning about highly leveraged firms: the breakeven sales point for a highly leveraged company is higher than the breakeven point for a company with less leverage. In the example above, for instance, the company increased the annual fixed charges it had to cover from $20,000 to $50,000 when it automated. Breakeven points for both operating structures are shown below.

Manual operation:

$$\frac{\$20,000 \text{ fixed cost}}{\$2 \text{ per unit contribution}} = 10,000\text{-unit breakeven point}$$

Automated operation:

$$\frac{\$50,000 \text{ fixed cost}}{\$4 \text{ per unit contribution}} = 12,500\text{-unit breakeven point}$$

In summary, operating leverage can improve a company's profits for a given level of sales, but to receive this benefit the company must endure the risk associated with an unstable profit pattern and an increased breakeven sales level.

Financial Leverage. A company uses financial leverage to increase the return to owners. The idea is very simple. Assume that investors are forming a company that requires an investment in assets of $100,000. The company is projected to yield earnings of $15,000 per year. If owners supply the entire $100,000, the return on owner's equity will be 15% (15,000/100,000).

Now assume instead that the owners wish to leverage their investment by borrowing half of the $100,000 required to start the business. Funds are available at 12% interest. If the owners follow this route, investing $50,000 and borrowing $50,000 at 12% interest, there will be an annual interest charge of $6,000 on the borrowed funds ($50,000 × .12), and earnings will be reduced to $9,000. But the owners' investment has been reduced from $100,000 to $50,000, and the return on owner's equity has been increased to 18% (9,000/50,000).

Red Flags. All companies use financial leverage to some extent. There is a great body of scholarly thought on just how great a proportion of a company's funding should come from debt and how much from owners. Too much debt increases business risk, and increased risk results in a company's having to pay higher interest rates on borrowed funds.

When interest rates are high, or return on assets is low, financial leverage may work against owners. Assume, for instance, in the illustration above, that the owners had to pay 20% interest on their borrowed $50,000. If the business does as expected and earns $15,000 before interest, the profit after an interest expense of $10,000 (50,000 × .20) will be only $5,000 and the return on owners' equity will be reduced to 10% (5,000/50,000).

Alternately, assume that the owners borrowed funds, as planned, at 12%, but that conditions changed and the company earned only $10,000 before the interest charges. After paying the $6,000 interest on the debt, profits would be only $4,000 and the return on owners' equity would be only 8% (4,000/50,000). If owners had not borrowed at all, the return on owners' equity would have been 10% (10,000/100,000).

Both operational and financial leverage can be used to benefit stockholders. But both can be dangerous if business conditions change drastically. Both forms of leverage maximize the benefit obtained from growth, but both may also maximize the damage that occurs when business slows.

The extent to which a company uses financial leverage can be determined by examining a company's debt structure and profit pattern. Since companies list their costs by function and not by behavior, however, it is very difficult to measure operating leverage directly.

49

COMMON SIZE STATEMENTS

Financial analysts sometimes use a variation of ratio analysis that looks at all the financial statement components. This method, called common size-statements, presents every item in a statement as a percentage of the largest item in the statement. Although this procedure may sound confusing, common size statements are in fact quite useful and easy to understand.

Both the income statement and the balance sheet can be converted to common size statements. The largest item in the income statement is sales. Thus, when the income statement is converted to a common size statement, all items in the income statement are expressed as percentages of sales. For instance, if cost of goods sold is 40% of sales, gross profit would then be 60% of sales. An illustration of a simple income statement converted to a common size statement is shown below.

INCOME STATEMENT

	Dollar Amounts	Common Size Amounts
Sales	$200,000	100%
Cost of Goods Sold	80,000	40%
Gross Profit	120,000	60%
Selling Expense	30,000	15%
Administrative Expense	50,000	25%
Operating Profit	40,000	20%
Income Taxes	20,000	10%
Net Income	$ 20,000	10%

Common size statements highlight the relationship of all the statement components. Common size statements are especially useful when two years of the company are compared side by side, or when two companies of different size are being compared.

When two years of the same company are being examined in common size form, changes in the relative size of the components will be apparent to the analyst—changes that might have been missed by someone examining only the absolute dollar amounts. For example, if sales have increased, an analyst might not notice that gross profit has decreased by several percentage points, or that selling costs have risen sharply as a percent of sales dollars. When the two years are converted to common size statements, both of those changes will be obvious.

Analyzing the financial statements of two companies of different size is more confusing than analyzing two years of the same company's statements. Large differences in the dollar amounts of the various expense items tend to camouflage differences in the relationship of the income statement components. Large differences in the proportion of the sales dollars spent on administrative expenses or debt service may go unnoticed if the statements are not converted to a common size format.

The largest item in the balance sheet is total assets, or total liabilities plus stockholders' equity. Thus, when a balance sheet is converted to a common size format, all components are expressed as percentages of total assets. For instance, current assets may be 40% of total assets. Bonds payable may be 30% of total liabilities plus stockholders' equity. (Remember that total assets and total liabilities plus stockholders' equity are equal. Either may be used.)

Red Flags. A variation of common size statements that is seen frequently is constructed using the financial statements of some prior year as the base, and expressing the components of all future years as percentages of each component in the base year. For instance, advertising in the base year may have been $10,000, then in the next three years, $11,000, $12,000, and $20,000, respectively. Expressed in common size as a percentage of the base-year amount of $10,000, advertising would appear as:

	Year 4	Year 3	Year 2	Year 1
Dollar Amount	$20,000	$12,000	$11,000	$10,000
Common Size Amount	200%	120%	110%	100%

The jump to 200% in year 4 appears significant, but the large percentage increase could be misleading. Advertising may be a $20,000 expense for a company with total expenses of $800,000. In such case, the small dollar amount involved—while a large percentage increase—may be immaterial. Investigation would be a waste of time.

50

FINANCIAL STATEMENT COMPARABILITY

Financial statement analysis is primarily a matter of making comparisons. A current ratio of 4:1 has no meaning by itself. It tells us only that current assets are four times current liabilities. But, if you find out that the company's current ratio for the past three years has been 2:1, 2:1, and 3:1, a pattern begins to emerge. (The current ratio is discussed in Key 46.)

For some reason, the current ratio is increasing. Is this good or bad? An excess of current assets is wasteful. Inventories may become obsolete. Receivable collections may be lax. On the other hand, too little invested in current assets relative to current liabilities is bad. Cash may not be available to pay creditors. Low inventory levels may cause stockouts. A comparison to prior years of the same company will help identify a trend but will not explain the cause or desirability of the pattern.

To determine the cause of an increase in the current ratio, we can look at the individual components of current assets and current liabilities. Most commonly, to determine the cause of an increase in the current ratio, we would look at the activity of accounts receivable and inventories. We might find that either accounts receivable turnover or inventory turnover had decreased because of larger balances in accounts receivable or more inventory stock on hand. A decrease in either of these ratios would help explain the increase in the current ratio. (Turnover ratios are discussed in Key 45.)

But even if we understand the cause of the current ratio increase to 4:1, we still do not know if 4:1 is good or bad. To assess the level of the current ratio, we must compare the company's ratio to ratios for other companies in the same industry. Composite ratios for different industries are published by Dun & Bradstreet, Standard & Poor's Corporation, Robert Morris Associates, and the Federal Trade Commission. These references can be found in most public or college libraries.

If we find that other companies in the same industry also have a composite current ratio of 4:1 (or close to it), we may feel that 4:1 is satisfactory. If we find that the industry current ratio is 2.5:1, we will be concerned by the increase from 2:1 to 4:1 over the last three years.

A company should always be analyzed by comparing its ratios (described in Keys 44-49) to the ratios of other companies in the same industry, or to the ratios of previous years in the same company. Comparisons to companies not in the same industry (comparing a bank to a paper mill) will generally have little meaning. You must remember that one ratio alone also generally has little meaning. You must calculate and compare ratios, measuring all facets of a company's activity and health (profitability, liquidity, activity, and solvency) if you are to make a clear analysis of the company's status. Understanding financial statements is no easy task. It requires hard work and diligence. It requires an inquisitive mind and proper preparation. You have begun by reading this book.

Good luck.

QUESTIONS AND ANSWERS

Q: *How should I use this book?*
A: This book is put to best use when you read it with an annual report at your side. There are many examples and illustrations throughout the text, but you will gain a special perspective if you either (1) read this book and, as each annual report component is covered, look it up in an annual report, or (2) read through the annual report of a company in which you are interested and, topic by topic, refer to this book as a reference to increase your understanding.

Q: *What are the types of audit opinions a CPA may issue?*
A: A CPA may issue an unqualified opinion, a qualified opinion, or an adverse opinion, or a CPA may disclaim an opinion. When CPAs believe the financial statements are fair presentations of the company's financial position and earnings for the year, they issue an unqualified or clean opinion. A qualified opinion points out the particular area the CPA believes is not fair presentation. An adverse opinion states that the CPA does not believe the financial statements are fairly presented. A disclaimer of opinion means that the CPA is not expressing an opinion on the financial statements.

Q: *Does an unqualified audit report mean that the CPA recommends the company as a good investment?*
A: No. It only means that the CPA believes the financial statements are fair presentations of the company's financial position and earnings for the year. This belief is based on tests the CPA conducts on samples of the company's records.

Q: *Does an unqualified audit report mean that the company's financial statements are free of error?*
A: No. CPAs plan their audits to try to detect all material

errors and irregularities. But their opinions are based on test samples of the company's records. Because they cannot test every record, it is possible that an error will go undetected.

Q: *Is a review the same as an audit?*
A: No. A review does not involve testing the accounting records from which the financial statements have been prepared. The CPA only questions management about the preparation of the financial statements and analyzes past and present financial statements to determine if unusual relationships exist. Where relationships appear normal the CPA does not investigate further. The review report will state that the CPA is not aware of any material changes needed to make the statements conform to generally accepted accounting principles. It will also state that the financial statements are unaudited.

Q: *Is Form 10-K the same as the annual report?*
A: No. Form 10-K must be filed with the SEC annually by publicly traded companies. While the 10-K contains the audited financial statements and much of the same information that companies include in their annual reports, it also contains additional, more detailed information.

Q: *How can I satisfy myself about a company's debt structure?*
A: The amount of a company's debt is generally shown under two classifications, current (or short-term) liabilities and noncurrent (or long-term) liabilities. Current liabilities are debts due in one year or less. The notes to the financial statements will contain a summary listing of noncurrent liabilities which gives the type, interest rate, and maturity date of each long-term debt. The level of a company's debt can be examined by calculating ratios of current assets to current liabilities and of noncurrent liabilities to total assets and comparing the results to the average ratios for the company's industry. Trends are also important. A "bad" ratio that is improving may be better than a deteriorating "good" ratio.

Q: *Where can I find industry average ratios?*

A: Industry average ratios are published by Dun & Bradstreet, Standard & Poor's, Robert Morris Associates, and the Federal Trade Commission. Most public or college libraries will have one or more sources of industry ratios.

Q: *Why is pension expense a significant part of many income statements?*

A: Reported pension expense is not the money paid to retirees during the year; more important, it represents the amount of money management should invest at the end of the year to cover future pension payments that are likely to be made to employees for this additional year's service. Management may choose to invest more or less than the current year's pension expense. Investing more than the current year's expense results in recording an asset, Prepaid Pension Cost. Investing less results in recording a liability, Unfunded Accrued Pension Cost. Actual payments to retirees are made from the pension fund investments.

Q: *Doesn't a balance sheet present the value of a business at a point in time?*

A: No. A balance sheet lists the resources and obligations of a business at a point in time. These resources and obligations are recorded at their original costs. No attempt is made to estimate the current values of the resources and obligations.

Q: *Is it always better for a company to have a great deal of cash on hand?*

A: No. Sometimes a company may wish to accumulate large cash balances in anticipation of acquiring another company or for some other reason, but in general there is an appropriate amount of cash for any company. Too much cash may indicate that management is not wisely investing in productive assets or retiring debt. Too little cash may cause problems as normal operating debts come due. The rule of thumb states that a company should have current assets equal to twice its current liabilities. The appropriate amount of cash varies for each industry, however. A diamond merchant may need large amounts of cash to conduct daily operations. A public utility will need very little cash in reserve, for that business is quite stable, with income and expenses pretty well balancing each other from month to month.

Q: *Why are there different methods to account for the same transaction? Is this to make it easy for companies to manipulate income?*

A: Different methods of accounting for the same transaction have developed over time as different accountants have looked at varying business practices and in good faith attempted to reflect the results of economic events in the accounts. Accountants may use several different methods of accounting for inventories and for productive assets depending on how the individual accountant believes the company has benefited from consuming the asset. Generally, straight-line depreciation (an equal amount each year) is used for assets from which the business benefits equally each year. An accelerated method of depreciation is used for assets that furnish most of their benefits during the early years of their lives. (A computer would probably be depreciated by an accelerated method.) The Financial Accounting Standards Board and others that set accounting standards attempt to resolve conflict when the choice between alternative accounting methods seems arbitrary.

Q: *Why are extraordinary items and discontinued operations shown separately in the income statement?*

A: Gains and losses that are not related to the main line of business or that occur infrequently are separately disclosed in order to allow comparisons of normal operating income between years. If we have an extraordinary gain this year and did not have one last year, it would only be appropriate to compare this year's income before extraordinary items to last year's net income.

Q: *What does it mean when a company labels its financial statements as "consolidated financial statements?"*

A: Consolidated financial statements are the combined statements of a parent company and its subsidiaries. Accounting principles require that the parent company combine the financial statements of its subsidiaries with its own when it owns more than 50% of the voting stock of the subsidiary.

Q: *What is the difference between an income statement and a statement of cash flows?*

A: An income statement shows the inflows and outflows of resources that result from earnings activities during the year. These inflows and outflows of resources may be different from the cash flows that result from operations. For example, sales may be made this year to a customer who will not pay until next year. The company records the sale as revenue earned in the year the sale was made. The statement of cash flows contains all inflows and outflows of cash whether from operations or other activities. A company may issue stock for cash or may buy equipment for cash. These transactions do not appear in the income statement but will be reported as sources and uses of cash in the statement of cash flows.

GLOSSARY

ACCELERATED DEPRECIATION method of depreciation that assumes more benefit is derived from a productive asset in the early years of its life. Less depreciation expense will be recorded each year of the asset's life. Sum of the years' digits and double-declining balance are examples of accelerated depreciation methods.

ACCOUNTING ENTITY business unit for which financial statements are being prepared. An accounting entity may be a complete business (such as a partnership or a corporation) or a smaller unit of business (such as a subsidiary or division).

ACCOUNTING PRINCIPLES BOARD (APB) formerly a unit of the American Institute of Certified Public Accountants (AICPA). Until the Financial Accounting Standards Board (FASB) was formed in 1973, APB was responsible for publishing opinions that formed the basis of Generally Accepted Accounting Principles.

ACCRUAL reporting concept that requires revenues to be reported in the fiscal period in which they are earned and expenses to be reported as they are incurred. Under the accrual concept, whether cash has been received or paid is irrelevant. *See also* Matching, Revenue recognition.

ADVERSE OPINION report issued by CPAs at the conclusion of an audit that states their opinion that the financial statements are not fair presentations of the company's financial position and earnings for the year.

ALLOWANCE FOR BAD DEBTS estimate of the dollar amount of accounts receivable that will not be collected, shown as a subtraction from total accounts receivable to calculate net (collectible) accounts receivable in the current assets section of the balance sheet.

AMERICAN INSTITUTE OF CERTIFIED PUBLIC ACCOUNTANTS (AICPA) professional association of certified public accountants.

AMORTIZATION assignment of the historical cost of an intangible asset to production periods as expense.

APB *see* Accounting Principles Board.

APPROPRIATED RETAINED EARNINGS portion of retained earnings not available for use in declaring dividends. When dividends are limited (as a creditor requirement, or to preserve cash for expansion), management may notify stockholders by appropriating a portion of retained earnings. (Alternatively, a restriction of dividends could be disclosed in the notes to the financial statements.)

ASSET anything of value that the business possesses and can use as it attempts to produce a profit.

AUDITOR'S OPINION report issued by CPAs at the conclusion of an audit. The report will state that based on the auditor's examination, the financial statements are or are not fair presentations of the company's financial position and earnings for the fiscal year. *See also* Adverse opinion, Disclaimer of opinion, Qualified opinion, Unqualified opinion

BALANCE SHEET financial statement that lists the assets, liabilities, and owner's equity of a business at a specific point in time.

BOND form of long-term debt, usually issued in $1000 increments, with interest paid semi-annually and the principal repaid in 10 or more years.

BOOK VALUE value at which an item is carried in the books and displayed in the balance sheet. The book value of a depreciable asset is the asset cost minus accumulated depreciation.

CAPITAL STOCK *see* Common stock.

CERTIFIED PUBLIC ACCOUNTANT (CPA) accountant who has passed a standardized examination and has met the experience and other requirements of one of the states. A CPA is licensed to audit financial statements and express an opinion as to their fairness.

COMMON STOCK ownership shares in a public corporation with the lowest preference as to assets on liquidation. Holders of common stock have the right to vote for the board of directors. In common usage, also called capital stock.

COMMON STOCK EQUIVALENT security convertible into common stock (as a convertible bond) or an option or warrant to purchase common stock.

COMPILATION procedure in which the CPA reads the financial statements and decides whether they are in proper form and appear to contain appropriate disclosures. The report issued will state that the CPA has not audited the financial statements and is not expressing an opinion on their fairness.

CONSERVATISM preference by accountants to place the lowest value on assets and income when faced with alternative valuations.

CONSOLIDATED FINANCIAL STATEMENT combined balance sheets, income statements, and statements of cash flows of a parent company and its subsidiaries.

CONTINGENCY situation where a company stands to gain or lose because of a past transaction or event. The amount of gain or loss will be determined by a later transaction or event. Thus, a law suit creates a contingency; the amount of gain or loss is dependent on a later event, the judgment.

CONTRIBUTED CAPITAL personal investment made by the owners of a business. Contributed capital plus retained earnings equals owners' equity.

CONVERSION PRIVILEGE agreement whereby a bond or a share of preferred stock may be exchanged for shares of common stock according to a predetermined formula.

CUMULATIVE DIVIDEND dividend agreement whereby a company must pay any dividends missed on preferred stock in past years before any dividend can be paid to common stockholders.

COST *see* Historical Cost, Period Cost, Product Cost.

CPA *see* Certified Public Accountant.

DEBENTURE long-term debt instrument not secured by any lien on a specific property.

DECLINING-BALANCE DEPRECIATION METHOD
see Accelerated depreciation.

DEFERRED TAX LIABILITY liability created when income reported on the income statement is not yet taxable but will become so in the future.

DEPLETION assignment of the historical cost of a natural resource to production periods as expense.

DEPRECIATION assignment of the historical cost of a long-lived productive asset to production periods as expense.

DISCLAIMER OF OPINION report issued by CPAs stating that they were not able to complete an audit and therefore are not expressing an opinion on the financial statements.

DONATED CAPITAL the value of an asset donated to a company is recorded and the source of the asset is shown as an increase in owners' equity called Paid-in Capital from Donations.

DOUBLE-DECLINING BALANCE DEPRECIATION
see Accelerated depreciation.

EXTRAORDINARY ITEM after-tax gain or loss on an unusual transaction that is not expected to reoccur.

FASB *see* Financial Accounting Standards Board.

FIFO *see* First in, first out.

FINANCIAL ACCOUNTING STANDARDS BOARD (FASB) independent board responsible for establishing accounting standards and concepts, founded in 1973 by the Financial Accounting Foundation as a successor to the Accounting Principles Board (APB).

FIRST IN, FIRST OUT (FIFO) method of accounting for inventory costs that assigns the costs of the most recently purchased units to inventory, and charges the cost of the oldest units to cost of goods sold. FIFO flows costs through a company the way most merchants flow products, selling the old units first.

FISCAL PERIOD financial reporting period that may cover a year (fiscal year) or a quarter (fiscal quarter).

FIXED ASSET *see* Property, plant and equipment.

GAAP *see* Generally Accepted Accounting Principles.

GENERALLY ACCEPTED ACCOUNTING PRIN-

CIPLES (GAAP) accounting profession's collection of rules governing financial statement presentation and measurement.

HISTORICAL COST total sum paid to purchase an asset and get it ready for use.

INCOME FROM CONTINUING OPERATIONS after-tax income of the portion of the business that is continuing.

INTANGIBLE ASSET long-lived productive asset that does not have a physical existence. Intangibles include patents, copyrights, trademarks and tradenames, franchises, organization costs, and purchased goodwill.

INTEREST COVERAGE *see* Times interest earned.

LAST IN, FIRST OUT (LIFO) method of accounting for inventory costs that assigns the costs of the most recently purchased units to cost of goods sold, and holds the cost of the oldest units in inventory.

LESSEE in a leasing arrangement, the party leasing the asset.

LESSOR in a leasing arrangement, the party providing the asset.

LIABILITY any debt of the business; the amounts owed to nonowners.

LIFO *see* Last in, first out.

MATCHING principle that tells the accountant when to record a production cost as expense. Costs directly associated with producing a certain revenue will be expensed in the same period that the revenue is recorded. Costs that benefit more than one period are expensed over the periods benefited.

MATERIALITY concept of relative importance. An item is material if it can influence a decision made by a user of the financial statements,. When an item is material, it must be accounted for within the measurement and reporting principles— Generally Accepted Accounting Principles.

NET ASSETS assets minus liabilities. Net assets are equal to owner's equity.

NET INCOME (LOSS) total of all reported revenues, gains, expenses, and losses for a fiscal period.

NONCURRENT LIABILITY any debt of the business that is not expected to be paid for at least one year from the date of the balance sheet.

OBLIGATION *see* Liability.

OPERATING CYCLE length of time required for a company to invest cash in inventory (by manufacture or purchase), sell the inventory, and collect the account receivable. The operating cycle is the sum of the accounts receivable turnover and the inventory turnover periods.

OPERATING LEASE leasing arrangement that does not transfer the risks of ownership to the lessee. The lessee will account for the lease payments as rental expense.

OVERHEAD all indirect manufacturing costs (in contrast to the direct costs of labor and materials)—depreciation, property taxes, insurance, energy, supervisory labor, etc.

OWNER'S EQUITY property rights of stockholders, calculated as assets minus liabilities; *see* Net assets.

PARENT COMPANY company that owns more than 50% of the voting stock of another company.

PENSION EXPENSE amount a company should invest at the end of the fiscal year to cover future pension payments that will be made to employees for this additional fiscal year's expense.

PERIOD COST nonmanufacturing cost, such as administrative expenses, that is expensed as time passes rather than becoming part of the cost of a manufactured product and being expensed when the product is sold.

PREEMPTIVE RIGHT right of common shareholders to maintain their proportionate ownership interest in a company by buying a like proportion of any new common stock issue.

PREFERRED STOCK class of stock that is preferred over common stock as to dividend distribution or asset distribution in liquidation. Preferred shareholders generally do not have the right to vote on the board of directors.

PREMIUM ON BOND PAYABLE difference between the face amount of a bond and the issue price when a bond is issued for more than face.

PREPAID PENSION COST asset created when a company invests more in its pension plan than the current year's pension expense.

PRICE EARNINGS RATIO market price of common stock divided by earnings per common share. This profitability ratio relates the market value of a company's common shares to the earnings per share of common stock.

PRODUCT COST manufacturing costs assigned to products produced and held as an asset until the product is sold. Product costs are expensed when products are sold. *See* Period costs.

PROPERTY, PLANT AND EQUIPMENT long-lived productive assets, such as land, buildings, machinery, and furniture and fixtures.

QUALIFIED OPINION report issued by CPAs at the conclusion of an audit that takes exception to the fairness of presentation of the financial statements. The report points out the particular area which the auditors believe is not fair presentation.

RECEIVABLE any claim a company has against others that are expected to be settled in cash. Receivables are either trade (customers' accounts and notes receivable) or nontrade (as tax refunds, employee advances, or dividends receivable).

RESOURCE *see* Asset.

RESULTS OF DISCONTINUED OPERATIONS after-tax gain or loss on a segment of the business that management intends to sell.

RETAINED EARNINGS dollar amount of assets furnished by earnings of the company that were not distributed as dividends.

REVENUE RECOGNITION revenue is reported in the fiscal period in which the sale is made (or the service is provided) regardless of whether cash is collected from the customer or the customer still owes for the merchandise (service).

REVIEW procedure in which a CPA analyzes past and present financial statements to determine if any unusual relationships exist. If there are none, the CPA will state that no material changes are needed to make the financial statements conform to Generally Accepted Accounting Principles. A review is not an audit.

SECURITIES AND EXCHANGE COMMISSION (SEC) federal agency created to administer the Securities Acts of 1933 and 1934. Although most accounting standards and concepts originated with the FASB or the APB, the SEC has final authority as to the accounting and reporting principles used in published annual reports.

SERIAL BONDS bonds that mature (come due) in increments, as an issue of bonds that is structured so that 20% of the bonds mature each year after the fifth year.

STATEMENT OF CASH FLOWS statement that reports all the changes that have occurred in the balance sheet during the fiscal period, either providing or using cash.

STATEMENT OF FINANCIAL POSITION *see* Balance sheet.

STRAIGHT-LINE DEPRECIATION method of depreciation that assumes equal benefit is derived from using a productive asset each year of its useful life. Depreciation expense will be the same each year under the straight-line method.

SUBSCRIBED STOCK a legally binding contract to purchase stock results in a receivable, Stock Subscriptions Receivable, and a component of owner's equity, Common Stock Subscribed. When the receivable is collected, the subscribed stock becomes simply common stock.

SUBSIDIARY COMPANY company in which more than 50% of the voting stock is owned by another company.

SUM OF THE YEARS' DIGITS DEPRECIATION *see* Accelerated depreciation.

TIMES INTEREST EARNED ratio of earnings before interest and taxes to interest expense. Sometimes called interest coverage. This ratio gives a measure of a company's ability to continue to service its debt if earnings decrease.

UNEARNED REVENUES Current liability created by collecting from customers before they receive the merchandise or services for which they are paying.

UNFUNDED ACCRUED PENSION COST liability created when a company invests less in its pension plan than the current year's pension expense.

UNFUNDED PROJECTED BENEFIT OBLIGATION
liability created when the current rate of earnings on the
invested pension plan assets is not enough to cover the future
benefits a company expects to pay the employees.

UNIT OF MEASURE currency being used in the financial
statements. For U.S. companies the unit of measure would be
the dollar, unadjusted for inflation or deflation.

UNITS OF PRODUCTION DEPRECIATION deprecia-
tion method that assumes benefit derived is directly related to
production. More depreciation expense would be recorded
for a year in which 10 million units were produced than for a
year in which 7 million units were produced.

UNQUALIFIED OPINION report issued by CPAs at the
conclusion of an audit stating their opinion that the financial
statements are fair presentations of the company's financial
position and earnings for the year. The accounting profession
views financial statements that follow Generally Accepted
Accounting Principles as being a fair presentation.

WEIGHTED AVERAGE INVENTORY method of accounting for inventory that assigns a weighted average cost
per unit to units in ending inventory and in cost of goods sold.

WORKING CAPITAL current assets minus current liabilities. Sometimes this refers to current assets alone.

INDEX